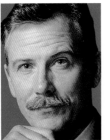    

Anton
Edelmann

Willi Elsener

Valentina Harris

Paul Heathcote

Ken Hom

Madhur Jaffrey

Simply the
BEST

SODEXHO

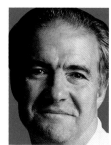

Alastair Little

Paul and
Jeanne Rankin

Gary Rhodes

Rick Stein

Franco Taruschio

Antony Worrall
Thompson

HarperCollins*Illustrated*

First published in 1998 by
HarperCollins*Publishers*, London, reprinted 1998

Compilation text copyright © Sodexho Alliance 1998
Food photographs copyright © HarperCollins*Publishers* 1998
Other photography copyright © Ivor Innes Ltd.; Caterer & Hotelkeeper; Sebastian Bone, Focal Point; William Levene Ltd; National Museum of Wales. Photograph of Franco Taruschio by Jean Cazals © BBC Worldwide Limited.

Registered office: Sodexho Alliance, Kenley House, Kenley Lane, Kenley, Surrey, CR8 5ED.

Editor: Jane Middleton
Photographer: Frank Weider
Assistant: Matthew Tugwell
Home Economist: Jane Lawrie
Stylist: Jo Harris
Indexer: Susan Bosanko

A catalogue record for this book is available from the British Library

ISBN 0 00 7646410

Typeset in Univers
Colour reproduction by Colourscan, Singapore
Printed and bound in Dubai

Wines kindly supplied by Michael Morgan Limited, London.

Sodexho Alliance and the Publishers wish to thank the undermentioned for permission to reproduce the following recipes. Master Class recipe titles may differ from the original recipe titles:

Anton Edelmann's recipes reprinted by permission of Pavilion Books from *Creative Cuisine* by Anton Edelmann, © Anton Edelmann.
'Cranberry & Baked Pear Pancakes with Calvados cream' reprinted by permission of Pavilion Books from *Music & Menus for Xmas* by Willi Elsener. 'Deep-fried sage leaves', 'Crisp tortellini in the Bolognese style', 'Lamb cutlets with proscuitto and mozzarella', 'Roast potatoes with lemon and rosemary', and 'Artichokes braised in the Roman style' reprinted from *Complete Italian Cookery Course* (BBC Books, Copyright © Valentina Harris 1992); 'Rolled pasta filled with ricotta and spinach' and 'Crisp ravioli with a sole filling' reprinted from *Perfect Pasta* (first published by Granada Publishing, Copyright © Valentina Harris 1984); 'Warm seafood salad of the Adriatic' reprinted from *Italian Regional Cookery* (BBC Books, Copyright © Valentina Harris 1990); 'Watermelon sorbet' reprinted from *Italian Family Feasts* (first published by Conran Octopus Ltd, Copyright © Valentina Harris 1990); 'Cassata Siciliana' reprinted from *Southern Italian Cookery* (first published by Grafton Books, Copyright © Valentina Harris 1990) by permission of Valentina Harris.
'Heathcote's black pudding', and 'Baked Christmas Alaska' reprinted by permission of Fourth Estate Ltd from Paul Heathcote's *Rhubarb and Black Pudding* by Matthew Fort © 1998 Matthew Fort and Paul Heathcote.
Ken Hom's recipes in Menu 1 reproduced from *Ken Hom's Hot Wok* with permission of BBC Worldwide Ltd © Ken Hom 1996. Recipes in Menu 2 reproduced from *Travels with a Hot Wok* with permission of BBC Worldwide Ltd © Ken Hom 1997, with the exception of 'Fried cucumber stuffed with pork' reproduced from *Illustrated Chinese Cookery* with permission of BBC Worldwide Ltd © Ken Hom 1996.
'Promila Kapoor's Paneer chat', and 'Nishrin Attarwala's Kari' reproduced from *Flavours of India* with permission of BBC Worldwide Ltd, © Madhur Jaffrey, 1994. 'Shorvedar Khumbi' and 'Sev ka murabba' reproduced with permission of BBC Worldwide Ltd, from *Quick & Easy Indian Cookery* © Madhur Jaffrey, 1993. 'Khatte meethe Baigan' and 'Bhagari Jhinga' reproduced from *Madhur Jaffrey's Spice Kitchen*, © Madhur Jaffrey, 1993 by Madhur Jaffrey. First published in Great Britain by Pavilion Books Ltd. Reprinted by permission of the author c/o Rogers, Coleridge & White Ltd., 20 Powis Mews, W11 1JN.
'Scallop and tiger prawn noodle salad' and 'Wrapped breast of chicken with cepes and truffles' reprinted by permission of Conran Octopus Ltd from *Keep it Simple* by Alastair Little, © 1993 Alastair Little and Richard Whittington.

'Torta di cioccolata' reprinted by permission of Random House UK Ltd from *Alastair Little's Italian Kitchen* by Alastair Little, published by Ebury Press, © 1996 Alastair Little. 'Fig and Frangipane Tart' reprinted from *Food of the Sun* © 1995 by Alastair Little and Richard Whittington, published by Quadrille.
'Blackened monkfish with curried aubergine' reprinted by permission of Reed Consumer Books Ltd from *Hot Food, Cool Jazz* by Paul and Jeanne Rankin, published by Mitchell Beazley (a division of Reed Consumer Books Ltd). 'Warm potato pancakes', 'Crispy Duck Confit' and 'Peppered leg of venison with hot and sour cabbage' reproduced from *Gourmet Ireland* by Paul and Jeanne Rankin with permission of BBC Worldwide Ltd, © Paul and Jeanne Rankin 1994. 'Roast guinea fowl with thyme, wild mushrooms' and 'Garlic bubble and squeak' reproduced from *Ideal Home Cooking*, published by Boxtree, © Paul and Jeanne Rankin 1998.
'Watercress, spinach and Parmesan salad with cider vinegar and mustard dressing', 'Roast chumps of lamb with spring greens and pickled red onions' reprinted by permission of David Higham Associates Ltd from *Open Rhodes Around Britain* by Gary Rhodes, published by BBC Books. 'Escalope of salmon with black treacle, juniper and sherry dressing', 'Chocolate banana bread pudding with chocolate sorber', and 'Tournedos of pork with caramelized apple and mashed potato sauce' reproduced from *Fabulous Food* with permission of BBC Worldwide Ltd, © Gary Rhodes 1997.
'Carpetshell clams with aioli', 'Panna cotta with fresh raspberries' and 'Spiny lobster with vanilla sauce' reproduced from *Fruits of the Sea* with permission of BBC Worldwide Ltd © Rick Stein 1997. 'Panache of scallops, squid and John Dory with a tomato, tarragon and chervil dressing' reproduced from *Rick Stein's Seafood Odyssey* with permission of BBC Worldwide Ltd © Rick Stein. 'Ceviche of monkfish with avocado' reproduced from *A Taste of the Sea* with permission of BBC Worldwide Ltd © Rick Stein 1995.
'Glamorgan sausages', and 'Cod with rosti and caponata marchigiani' reproduced from *Franco & Friends* with permission of BBC Worldwide Ltd © Franco Taruschio 1997. 'Crescente' reproduced from *Bruschetta, Crostoni and Crostini* with permission of Pavilion Books, © Franco Taruschio. 'Roast best end of lamb with wild mushrooms' and 'Baked polenta with ricotta' reproduced from *Leaves from the Walnut Tree* with permission of Pavilion Books, © Franco Taruschio. 'Pasta torte' and 'Timpano di lasagne al duca d'este' reproduced from *Pasta al forno*, published by Pavilion Books, © Franco Taruschio 1998.

Sodexho Alliance have used their best endeavours to ensure permission has been sought for all recipes used where necessary.

Foreword

Sodexho Alliance has an absolute passion for food and the Master Class series fuels this passion. We owe it to our clients and customers alike to keep our ideas and menus fresh and exciting, balancing and monitoring the quality of ingredients with nutrition and flavour.

Master Class was born from our constant desire to be at the leading edge of food service. We invite the most respected and innovative chefs to train and direct our people. The consequent development of their skills and techniques leads me to believe there has never been a more rewarding time to be a chef with Sodexho Alliance. As Master Class has evolved it has inspired us all to a greater understanding of food. This book is a compilation of the menus and recipes featured in the Master Class programme.

Britain has become a melting pot of recipe ideas from around the world. Experimentation has been welcomed, with restaurants drawing influence from the world of design, music and art, stimulating every sense and heightening the dining experience.

Modern lifestyles don't always afford us the opportunity to enjoy dining as we should. Please use this book to redress the balance. Whether it is Italian or fusion food that excites you, Thai influences or modern British, the most important thing is that you take some time to prepare the dishes and enjoy sharing them with friends.

Bon appétit.

David Ford
Chief Executive
Sodexho

Contents

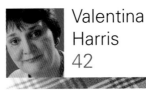

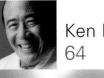

Introduction

The background

I trained as a chef at a time when it was unfashionable to cook. The UK had taken the world by storm with pop music but not, alas, gastronomy. Well, I'm delighted to have witnessed the positive change in the UK and we can be proud of the quality and diversity of food at all levels today – from hotels and restaurants to staff canteens. Specialist food shops and supermarkets bring high-quality ingredients within arm's reach of home cooks, giving them the opportunity to produce excellent food. The chefs in this book have contributed significantly to the new food culture. They are true masters of their profession and produced wonderful Master Classes.

The Master Class programme

Over 300 Sodexho Alliance chefs have attended a Master Class and worked with one of their culinary heroes. The format of the series is simple: together with our chosen Master Chef we devise a menu that reflects a particular theme and embodies his or her philosophy of food. We invite up to 15 chefs to take part in the Master Class. On the day of the programme, the Master Chef demonstrates the dishes and then our chefs prepare them under his or her supervision. In the evening, to celebrate the occasion, we invite some of the chefs' clients to sample the fruits of their labours and our Master Chef joins us to explain each course to the guests. One of our chefs told me his Master Class was simply the best day of his life, and this is where the title of this book came from.

The venues

The venues chosen for the Master Class programme are all places where we, as contract caterers, are delighted to provide the catering service, with the exception of Kenley House, which is our own international residential training centre. Each location adds a special element to the whole Master Class experience.

The Master Chefs

There are certain qualities shared by all of these great chefs – they are creative, adventurous, passionate, positive, and gifted communicators. They have all played a great part in raising the standard of food available in this country.

Anton Edelmann

Maître Chef des Cuisines at The Savoy Hotel, Anton is not only one of the most respected chefs in the land he is also a great teacher. Everyone who has worked on his Master Classes is delighted by the amount of time he devotes to each individual.

Willi Elsener

Maître Chef des Cuisines at The Dorchester Hotel, Willi uses influences from the global kitchen. His precision and planning are object lessons to anyone who has to produce food in large quantities. A thoughtful chef, with many wonderful ideas.

Valentina Harris

Valentina has a passionate approach to cooking genuine Italian food – not just classic restaurant dishes but also the whole gambit of Italian cooking from the regions. She is a great teacher and a fabulous storyteller, which adds to the magic she creates.

Paul Heathcote

One of the new breed of chefs, Paul has great culinary vision and an infectious enthusiasm for food. He calls on his native north-west for inspiration in terms of recipes and ingredients.

Ken Hom

Ken has influenced so many by his mastery of Chinese food. He also brings to his cooking a wealth of knowledge of global cuisines and creates exciting fusions from different cultures.

Madhur Jaffrey

Madhur has demystified Indian food and helped us understand how to use and combine spices. She entranced our chefs throughout her Master Class in Scotland.

Alastair Little

Alastair's keep-it-simple approach and breadth of knowledge about Mediterranean cooking make a powerful combination. He also has a great sense of humour.

Paul and Jeanne Rankin

Two for the price of one: Paul, who has an intensity about food and flavour, and Jeanne, whose desserts are just delightful. Their travels around the world have brought a unique quality to their cuisine.

Gary Rhodes

Gary is a real innovator who has probably done more for British food in the last four years than anyone else. He has reworked classic dishes, always improving on the original, and created unique dishes of his own.

Rick Stein

Man of the sea, Rick brings a passion and understanding to seafood that are unequalled. If in Padstow, don't miss his Seafood Restaurant.

Franco Taruschio

Franco has spent over 30 years producing wonderful food at The Walnut Tree Inn in Wales. He combines influences from his native Italy with the local produce of Wales, plus a hint of Thai flavours – a culinary genius.

Antony Worrall Thompson

Antony is in the vanguard of the new wave of chefs who wanted to challenge the old order and create a new food culture.

I thank them all for contributing to this unique collection of recipes and for the great fun and pleasure they have brought to Master Class. It is a real privilege working with such great talent.

How the book works

Each chapter represents the menu of a Master Class (two menus in some cases), each devised to serve four or six people. The suggested wines are the ones we served with the menus; you may wish to find similar wines for your entertaining. The final chapter contains dishes that you could use over the Christmas period to add to your festive fun. For the best results, always select and use the very best ingredients.

The charity

All my colleagues and collaborators on this book have benefited from the catering industry, so to give a little help to those in need a donation for every copy sold will be made to the Hotel and Catering Benevolent Fund.

And finally ... I would like to thank the members of the Sodexho Alliance team who have worked with me on bringing this book together. For all his work on Master Class and the book, John Whybrew, with invaluable assistance from Lynne Morrison, Peter Joyner, Vicci Field, Amanda Snow, Julia Newton, Julia Cohen, Pam Allen and Claire Day.

Also, I must thank everyone at HarperCollins and their team for their patience and help.

Good food enriches lives – enjoy!

Peter Hazzard

Peter Hazzard
Executive Director – Food Services,
Sodexho

Introduction

Anton Edelmann's culinary career has taken him through Switzerland, Belgium and Germany. After working with Anton Mosimann at the Dorchester, he oversaw the opening of the Grosvenor House Hotel's prestigious restaurant, Ninety Park Lane. He is currently *Maître Chef des Cuisines* at The Savoy Hotel in London, where he has gained many accolades, including the 1991 *Caterer & Hotelkeeper* Chef of the Year Award. He regularly travels as a consultant chef to the USA, Thailand and Japan.

Anton Edelmann's books include *Christmas Feast*, *Fast Feasts*, *The Savoy Food and Drink Book*, *Creative Cuisine* and *Perfect Pastries, Puddings and Desserts*.

Anton Edelmann

Anton Edelmann
cooks at Kenley House

"The Kenley training kitchens provided the ideal environment for me to carry out my Master Class. I was determined that the chefs enjoyed the day as much as the diners."

menu 1

serves 4

Langoustines in their pyjamas
   with mango sauce

Navarin of lamb with couscous
Grilled vegetables

Orange quark soufflé

wine suggestions

Pinot Blanc 1993

Cabernet Shiraz 1994 South Australia

Maury

Langoustines in their pyjamas with mango sauce

ingredients

16 raw langoustines
(or large prawns)

16 squares of filo pastry, each
10 × 10 cm/4 × 4 inches

melted unsalted butter for brushing

32 large fresh basil leaves

1 egg yolk, beaten

vegetable oil for deep-frying

4 handfuls of mixed salad leaves,
weighing about 90 g/3¼ oz

sea salt and freshly ground
black pepper

FOR THE MANGO SAUCE:

1 large ripe mango, peeled, stoned
and coarsely chopped

1 hard-boiled egg yolk

4 tablespoons mayonnaise

2 teaspoons finely shredded
fresh basil

FOR THE SOY DRESSING:

60 ml/2 fl oz orange juice

1½ teaspoons white wine vinegar

1½ teaspoons soy sauce

2 tablespoons olive oil

First make the mango sauce: put the mango flesh in a food processor or blender with the hard-boiled egg yolk and mayonnaise and work until smooth. Press the mixture through a fine sieve into a bowl. Stir in the shredded basil and season to taste with salt and pepper. Set the sauce aside.

Next make the soy dressing: put the orange juice in a small saucepan and boil until reduced to ½ tablespoon. Leave to cool completely, then whisk well with all the remaining ingredients and season to taste with black pepper. Set aside.

Shell the langoustines, then make a shallow cut down the rounded back of each one and remove the dark intestinal vein. Rinse the langoustines and pat dry with kitchen paper. Season with salt and pepper.

Put a filo square on the work surface and brush it with melted butter. Set a basil leaf in the centre and put a langoustine on top. Brush the edges of the filo with a little beaten egg yolk. Fold 2 opposite sides of the square over the langoustine and press to seal. Wrap and seal the remaining langoustines in the same way.

Heat a pan of oil for deep-frying to 165–175°C/330–345°F. Add the langoustines in filo, 4 at a time. Fry for 3 minutes or until golden and crisp, turning them over a few times so that they brown evenly. Drain on kitchen paper. When you have fried all the langoustines, raise the temperature of the oil to 180°C/350°F. Add the remaining basil leaves and fry for a few seconds until crisp, bright green and translucent, then drain.

Toss the salad leaves in the soy dressing, then divide them between 4 serving plates, piling them up in a mound. Arrange the langoustines in filo on the plates and garnish with the fried basil. Serve with the mango sauce.

Navarin of lamb with couscous

ingredients

8 middle neck lamb chops

3 tablespoons groundnut oil

1 large onion, roughly chopped

1 carrot, roughly chopped

5 garlic cloves, roughly chopped

1 leek, white and pale green
parts only, chopped

3 tablespoons tomato purée

300 ml/½ pint red wine

2 tablespoons flour

750 ml/1¼ pints well-flavoured
chicken stock

1 fresh thyme sprig

1 fresh marjoram sprig

salt and freshly ground
black pepper

FOR THE COUSCOUS:

3 tablespoons groundnut oil

1 onion, finely chopped

2 'nests' of vermicelli

50 g/2 oz livers from chicken,
turkey or game birds, cleaned and
cut into bite-sized pieces if large

100 g/4 oz flaked almonds,
coarsely chopped

150 ml/¼ pint dry white wine

250 ml/8 fl oz well-flavoured
chicken stock

2.5 cm/1 inch piece of
cinnamon stick

250 g/9 oz couscous

chopped fresh flat-leaf parsley,
to garnish (optional)

salt and freshly ground
black pepper

Season the lamb with salt and pepper. Heat a flameproof casserole over a high heat and add the oil. Brown the lamb chops briskly on both sides, then remove and set aside. Add the onion, carrot, garlic and leek and cook over a moderately low heat until lightly browned, stirring often. Add the tomato purée and cook for 30 seconds, stirring well. Add one third of the wine, stir well and bring to the boil. Boil until the wine is reduced to a thick glaze. Repeat with the remaining wine, adding it in 2 batches. Add the flour and stir well for 1 minute, then gradually stir in the chicken stock. Bring to the boil. Add the herbs and some salt and pepper, then return the lamb to the casserole. Cover and transfer to an oven preheated to 180°C/350°F/Gas Mark 4. Braise for about 2 hours or until the lamb is very tender, stirring occasionally.

Meanwhile, prepare the couscous. Heat the oil in a saucepan over a low heat and cook the onion until soft and translucent, stirring often. Crush the vermicelli finely and add to the pan. Stir over medium heat until golden brown. Add the livers, almonds and wine and bring to the boil. Simmer for 1 minute. Add the chicken stock, cinnamon and some salt and pepper and bring back to the boil. Add the couscous and stir for 1 minute. When the mixture returns to the boil, reduce the heat to very low, cover the pan and simmer for 10–15 minutes or until the couscous is tender and all the liquid has been absorbed. Remove the pan from the heat and set aside, covered, for 5 minutes. Discard the cinnamon, fluff the couscous grains, then taste and adjust the seasoning. If you like, fold in some chopped parsley before serving.

Remove the lamb chops from the casserole and keep warm. Strain the sauce through a fine sieve, pressing down on the vegetables and seasonings to extract the maximum flavour and liquid, then taste and adjust the seasoning. Spoon the sauce over the lamb and serve with the couscous and Grilled vegetables (see opposite) – or with a selection of baby vegetables if you prefer (see pages 26–7).

Grilled vegetables

ingredients

2 small heads of garlic

1 small kohlrabi, peeled and cut into rounds about 3 mm/⅛ inch thick

2 courgettes, cut lengthways into slices about 3 mm/⅛ inch thick

1 aubergine, cut lengthways into slices about 5 mm/¼ inch thick, or 4 baby aubergines, left whole

100 ml/3½ fl oz olive oil

1 red and 1 green pepper, deseeded and cut into triangles about 6 cm/ 2½ inches long

2–3 fresh rosemary sprigs

2–3 fresh thyme sprigs

salt and freshly ground black pepper

Cut each head of garlic horizontally in half. Put the halves cut-side up in a pan of cold water, bring to the boil and boil for 1 minute. Drain, then repeat this blanching twice. Drain well.

Put the kohlrabi, courgette and aubergine slices (if using a large aubergine) on a large tray and sprinkle generously with salt and pepper. Set aside for 5 minutes to draw out the liquid, then pat dry with kitchen paper.

Heat the grill and grill pan with rack in place, or heat a ridged cast iron grill pan on top of the stove, until it is very hot. Pour the olive oil into a roasting pan or baking tray, turn all the vegetables in the oil to coat, then transfer them to the hot grill rack or pan. Grill them quickly on both sides until they are tender and golden brown: the kohlrabi and garlic will take about 10 minutes, the aubergine and peppers 7–10 minutes and the courgettes 4–5 minutes.

Return the vegetables to the pan of oil and add the herbs. Set aside until needed. Just before serving, warm the grilled vegetables in the oven or under the grill.

Orange quark soufflé

If the quark is very wet, squeeze it well through a muslin or omit one egg yolk.

ingredients

4 oranges

a little caster sugar for sprinkling

2 large eggs, separated

285 g/10 oz quark

finely grated zest of 1
unwaxed lemon

5 teaspoons cornflour

2 tablespoons light rum

6 tablespoons icing sugar

1 large egg white

300 ml/½ pint freshly squeezed
orange juice

4 fresh mint sprigs, to decorate

**FOR THE CARAMELIZED
ORANGE ZEST:**

2 unwaxed oranges

150 g/5 oz sugar

100 ml/3½ fl oz water

grenadine (optional)

First prepare the caramelized orange zest (this can be done well in advance). Pare the zest very thinly from the oranges, being careful not to take off any of the white pith. Cut the zest into very thin strips and blanch in a pan of boiling water for 30 seconds, then drain. Put the sugar and water in a saucepan (or use half water and half grenadine). Bring slowly to the boil, stirring to dissolve the sugar. Add the strips of zest and simmer for about 10 minutes or until the sugar syrup has reduced by about half. Remove from the heat and leave to cool. Leave the zest in the sugar syrup until ready to use.

Peel the oranges, removing all the white pith, and cut out the segments from between the membranes. Set aside. Butter 4 individual soufflé dishes and sprinkle them with sugar.

Mix together the egg yolks, quark, lemon zest, half the cornflour, the rum and half the icing sugar. In a separate bowl, whisk the 3 egg whites with the remaining icing sugar until they form stiff peaks. Stir a spoonful of the whites into the quark mixture to loosen it, then gently fold in the remaining whites with a large metal spoon. Divide the soufflé mixture between the prepared dishes. Put the dishes in a roasting tin and pour enough cold water into the tin to come half way up the sides of the dishes. Bake in an oven preheated to 220°C/425°F/Gas Mark 7 for 15 minutes or until well risen and golden.

Meanwhile, mix the remaining cornflour with 2 tablespoons of the orange juice. Strain the remaining juice into a saucepan and heat, then stir in the cornflour mixture. Simmer, stirring, until thickened. Just before serving, add the orange segments and heat through.

Remove the orange segments and arrange them around the edges of 4 serving plates. When the soufflés are done, remove them from the tin of water. Holding each dish in a towel, loosen the sides of the soufflé with a small sharp knife and turn it out upside down in the centre of a plate. Spoon the orange sauce around the soufflés. Scatter over the caramelized zest, decorate with a sprig of mint and serve immediately.

Anton Edelmann
cooks at
North West Water

"I always enjoy Master Class because the chefs respond well and I appreciate the challenge of a different kitchen!"

menu 2

serves 4

Chargrilled brill fillet with asparagus
and a warm tomato herb dressing

Fillet of beef with pesto and
Mediterranean vegetable ragout
Pommes savoyardes
Selection of seasonal
baby vegetables

Warm cherry tart with cinnamon ice
cream and raspberry sauce

Chocolate pralines

wine suggestions

Ayala Château d'Ay Brut

Santa Rita Reserva Chardonnay 1994

Best Great Western Shiraz,
Concongella Vineyard 1991

Château Coutet, 1er Cru Classé Barsac
1989

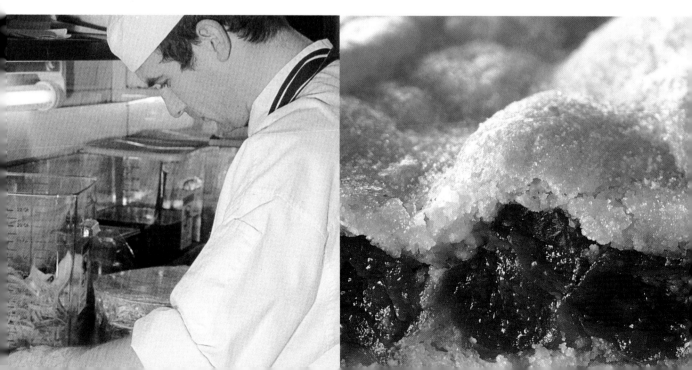

Chargrilled brill fillet with asparagus and a warm tomato herb dressing

ingredients

16 small asparagus spears or 24 asparagus tips

4 pieces of skinless brill fillet or other flat fish, weighing about 150 g/5 oz each

2 tablespoons vegetable oil

a little unsalted butter

4 teaspoons balsamic vinegar

sea salt and freshly ground black pepper

FOR THE TOMATO HERB DRESSING:

125 ml/4 fl oz olive oil

2 tablespoons sherry vinegar

200 g/7 oz ripe but firm plum tomatoes, peeled, deseeded and finely diced

4 tablespoons chopped fresh mixed herbs, such as chives, parsley, basil and dill

Prepare and cook the asparagus as described on page 26.

Heat a ridged cast-iron grill pan until it is very hot. Season the fish with salt and pepper, then turn it in the oil to coat. Set the pieces of fish on the grill pan, then after about 25 seconds give them a half-turn to mark a criss-cross pattern. Repeat on the other side. Cover the fish with buttered paper and transfer to an oven preheated to 200°C/400°F/Gas Mark 6. Cook for about 5 minutes or until the fish is opaque. Test with the point of a knife: the flesh in the centre should still be slightly translucent.

Meanwhile, put the asparagus in a pan with a little butter and 1 tablespoon of water and heat until the water has evaporated and the asparagus is hot. Season with salt and pepper.

For the dressing, put the olive oil and sherry vinegar in a pan and heat until lukewarm, stirring constantly (do not allow it to boil). Stir in the tomatoes and herbs and season to taste.

Place the fish on warmed plates and give it a turn of the peppermill. Pour around the tomato and herb dressing. Arrange the asparagus around the fish and sprinkle everything with the balsamic vinegar. Serve immediately.

menu 2 Anton Edelmann

Fillet of beef with pesto and Mediterranean vegetable ragout

ingredients

4 fillet steaks, weighing about
150 g/5 oz each

3 tablespoons vegetable oil

4 large flat mushrooms

20 g/¾ oz unsalted butter

4 tablespoons pesto sauce

4 teaspoons freshly grated
Parmesan cheese

fresh rosemary sprigs, to garnish

salt and freshly ground
black pepper

FOR THE MEDITERRANEAN VEGETABLE RAGOUT:

2 red peppers

100 ml/3½ fl oz olive oil

1 onion, finely chopped

2 garlic cloves, crushed to a paste

100 g/4 oz mushrooms, cut into
quarters

2 courgettes, cut into
1 cm/½ inch cubes

1 small fresh rosemary sprig

½ teaspoon sugar

½ teaspoon white wine vinegar

4 ripe but firm plum tomatoes,
peeled, deseeded and cut into
1 cm/½ inch squares

First prepare the Mediterranean vegetable ragout. Rub the red peppers with a little of the olive oil and put them in a small casserole or roasting tin. Cover with a lid or foil and bake in an oven preheated to 220°C/425°F/Gas Mark 7 for 20 minutes. Remove from the oven and set aside, covered, for 10 minutes. Reduce the oven temperature to 180°C/350°F/Gas Mark 4. When the peppers are cool enough to handle, peel them, discard the white ribs and seeds and cut the flesh into 1 cm/½ inch squares.

Heat the remaining olive oil in a flameproof casserole and cook the onion over a low heat until soft and translucent, stirring often. Add the garlic and cook for 1 minute longer. Add the mushrooms and courgettes and cook for 2 minutes, stirring occasionally. Add the red peppers and stir well. Add the rosemary, sugar and vinegar and season with salt and pepper. Cover the casserole, transfer to the oven and cook for 25 minutes, stirring frequently. Stir in the tomatoes, then taste and adjust the seasoning.

For the steaks, heat the grill and the grill pan with the rack in place. Season the steaks with salt and pepper and turn them in the oil to coat. Arrange them on the hot grill rack and grill until they are cooked according to taste, turning them over once.

Meanwhile, remove the stalks from the mushrooms. When the steaks have been turned over, season the mushrooms, turn them in the oil and arrange them curved-side up on the rack with the steaks. Grill until lightly browned. Turn them over and put one-quarter of the butter into each cap. Continue grilling until tender.

Put a mushroom, curved-side down, on each steak. Spread pesto sauce on the mushrooms and sprinkle with the Parmesan. Return to the grill, close to the heat, for about 10 seconds, just to brown the top lightly.

Divide the vegetable ragout among 4 warmed serving plates, arranging it in a ring in the centre. Set the steaks on top and give them a turn of the pepper mill. Garnish with the rosemary sprigs and serve.

Pommes savoyardes

ingredients

300 g/10½ oz potatoes

20 g/¾ oz unsalted butter

2 tablespoons oil

salt and freshly ground
black pepper

Peel the potatoes and trim them into neat cylinder shapes. Cut them into slices about 3 mm/⅛ inch thick and then dry thoroughly on a kitchen cloth. Use the butter to grease 4 round 10 cm/4 inch tins.

Heat the oil in a pan and toss the potato slices very quickly in it to blanch them. Season generously with salt and pepper, then arrange neatly in the buttered tins. Place the tins directly over a high heat for 2–3 minutes to brown the base, then bake in an oven preheated to 200°C/400°F/Gas Mark 6 for about 20 minutes or until the potatoes are tender. Unmould to serve.

Selection of seasonal baby vegetables

Baby vegetables are tender so they need only brief cooking. Select 3 or 4 types from the ones suggested below so you have a good combination of colours. You will need 450–600 g/1–1¼ lb in total to serve 4. Cook each vegetable separately, ahead of time if that is convenient, then finish for serving as described opposite.

BABY ASPARAGUS

When in season, tender young asparagus spears need only have the 'leaves' on the sides of the stalks removed with a knife or vegetable peeler. If the ends of the stalks are woody, however, trim them off, then lay each spear on a chopping board and scrape the skin off the whole length of the stalk, working away from the tip. Cook in simmering salted water for 2½ minutes or until just tender but still firm. Drain and refresh in iced water, then drain again well.

BABY BEETROOT

Cook whole beetroot in simmering salted water for 10–12 minutes or until just tender but still firm. Drain well and refresh under cold running water, then peel.

BABY CARROTS

Scrub or peel, leaving on a little of the green end. Melt some butter in a small saucepan and add a pinch of sugar and the carrots. Cook over a moderate heat for 3 minutes, stirring often. Add 5–6 tablespoons of water and season with salt and pepper. Cover the pan and cook over a very low heat for about 6 minutes or until the carrots are tender but still have some bite.

BABY CAULIFLOWER

Trim off most of the leaves and the base of the core. Cook in simmering salted water for about 4 minutes or until just tender but still firm. Drain and refresh in iced water, then drain again well.

BABY COURGETTES

Trim the ends. Cook in simmering salted water for about 3 minutes or until just tender but still firm. Drain and refresh in iced water, then drain again well.

SMALL BUTTON MUSHROOMS

Trim the stalks. Melt a little butter in a small saucepan, add the mushrooms and season with salt and pepper. Cover and cook over a moderately low heat for 2 minutes.

BUTTON OR BABY ONIONS

Peel, then cook in simmering salted water for 4–5 minutes or until tender but still firm. Drain and refresh in iced water, then drain again well.

FRESH PEAS

If very small, leave in the pod. Otherwise, shell them. Cook in simmering salted water for 2–3 minutes or until just tender but still firm. Drain and refresh in iced water, then drain again well.

BABY TURNIPS

Use only small ones, as large turnips have an inferior flavour. Scrub or peel, leaving a little of the green end attached. Melt some butter in a small saucepan and add a pinch of sugar and the turnips. Cook over a moderate heat for 3 minutes, stirring often. Add 5–6 tablespoons of water and season with salt and pepper. Cover the pan and cook over a low heat for 10 minutes or until the turnips are just tender but still have some bite.

TO FINISH

Warm carrots in their cooking liquid. Heat beetroot separately in butter. Toss all the other vegetables in hot butter. Season with salt and pepper and serve.

Warm cherry tart
with cinnamon ice cream
and raspberry sauce

ingredients

225 g/8 oz plain flour

1 teaspoon baking powder

½ teaspoon salt

100 g/4 oz cold unsalted butter, cut into cubes

100 g/4 oz caster sugar

finely grated zest of 1 unwaxed lemon

1 egg

500 g/1 lb 2 oz fresh cherries, stoned

a little egg white

200 ml/7 fl oz plain yoghurt

shavings of cinnamon stick, to decorate (optional)

FOR THE CINNAMON ICE CREAM:

1.25 litres/2¼ pints double cream

2½ very fresh cinnamon sticks

200 ml/7 fl oz milk

6 egg yolks

75 g/3 oz caster sugar

3 tablespoons liquid glucose

FOR THE RASPBERRY SAUCE:

300 g/10½ oz raspberries

2 teaspoons lemon juice

40 g/1½ oz icing sugar

First make the ice cream. Put 1 litre/1¾ pints of the cream in a pan with the cinnamon and boil until reduced by half. Strain and leave to cool. Bring the remaining cream and the milk to the boil. Beat the egg yolks with the sugar until pale and thick. Pour the cream and milk on to the yolks, whisking well, then return the mixture to the pan and cook very gently, stirring continuously, until it is thick enough to coat the back of the spoon. Remove from the heat and pass through a fine sieve, then mix in the glucose. Leave to cool, then stir in the cinnamon cream.

Freeze in an ice-cream machine until firm. If you don't have an ice-cream machine, pour the mixture into a shallow bowl, cover and freeze for 2 hours, until it begins to firm up. Transfer to a blender or food processor and whizz until the ice crystals have broken down. Pour back into the bowl, cover and return to the freezer for 2 hours. Repeat twice, then freeze until firm.

To make the tart, sift the flour, baking powder and salt into a bowl. Rub in the butter. Add all but 1 tablespoon of the sugar, plus the lemon zest and egg and mix to form a dough. Wrap in clingfilm and chill for 1 hour. Roll out two-thirds of the dough to a thickness of 5 mm/ ¼ inch and use to line a buttered 15 cm/6 inch flan ring placed on a baking sheet (or a loose-bottomed flan tin). Pack the cherries in tightly, pressing them firmly into the dough. Roll out the remaining dough and place it on top. Cut off excess dough, then press the edges gently down inside the ring to seal. Chill for 20 minutes, then brush the top with egg white and sprinkle with the reserved sugar. Bake the tart in an oven preheated to 190°C/ 375°F/Gas Mark 5 for 25 minutes or until golden brown. Cool slightly, then remove the flan ring or side of the tin.

For the sauce, purée the raspberries, lemon juice and icing sugar, then press through a fine sieve.

Transfer the ice cream to the fridge 20–30 minutes before serving to soften slightly. Serve the tart with the raspberry sauce and yoghurt and a scoop of ice cream – decorated with shavings of cinnamon if desired.

Chocolate pralines

Makes about 20

ingredients

small amount of dry ice (optional)

100 g/3½ oz ice cream of your choice (mint-chocolate and vanilla are especially good, but don't use soft-scoop), frozen until very firm

100 g/3½ oz luxury white chocolate, chopped

125 ml/4 fl oz double cream

100 g/3½ oz luxury plain chocolate, chopped

Place a small baking tray lined with baking parchment over the dry ice, if using. With a small melon baller, shape small balls of ice cream and place on the tray to harden. Stick a cocktail stick into each one before it hardens. (If you don't have any dry ice, place the baking tray lined with parchment in the freezer until very cold, then remove and place the ice-cream balls on it; return to the freezer while you melt the chocolate.)

Place the white chocolate in a small bowl with 4 tablespoons of the cream. Place the plain chocolate in a small bowl with the remaining cream. Melt both over a saucepan of simmering water and stir until smooth.

Dip half the ice-cream balls in the dark chocolate mixture one at a time and return to the baking tray immediately to harden. Dip the remaining ice cream balls in the white chocolate. Store in the freezer in a rigid container until required.

For a dramatic presentation place a small amount of dry ice in a bowl and pour a little boiling water on to it. This forms a 'mist'. Set the pralines on a plate and place on the bowl of dry ice. Serve immediately.

Alternatively, serve the chocolate balls on crushed ice.

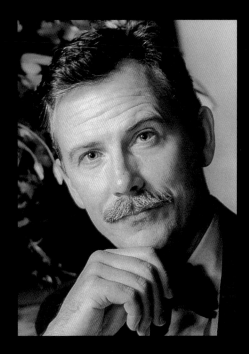

Willi Elsener was born into a family of Swiss hoteliers and has worked in some of Switzerland's major hotels, winning his country's top gastronomic honour, the Diplôme de Cuisinier, when he was only 26. Since 1986 he has been Executive Chef of The Dorchester Hotel in London, where he has revitalized traditional British cooking in the Grill Room, picking up a succession of awards in the process, and created the Oriental Restaurant, currently the only Chinese restaurant in the UK to hold a Michelin star.

Willi Elsener is the author of *A World of Flavours* and *Music and Menus for Christmas*.

Willi Elsener

Willi Elsener
cooks at
Blenheim Palace

"I wanted to replicate the food from The Dorchester within the splendid confines of Blenheim Palace."

menu

serves 4

Spring roll basket with crab
  meat and smoked salmon

Pan-fried scallops served on tomato
  confit flavoured with black beans

Oven-roasted quail breast with
  green mango and potato cake

Baked escalope of sea bass
  flavoured with lime and coriander
  and a port wine sauce

Apple and cinnamon cake served
  with Calvados ice cream

wine suggestions

Bel Arbor Sauvignon Blanc 1994

Chianti Classico Riserva,
  Terre della Fortezza 1991

Aloxe Corton Louis Jadot 1989

Château Climens, Barsac,
  1er Cru Classé 1985

Spring roll basket with crab meat and smoked salmon

Willi Elsener

ingredients

1 large sheet of spring roll pastry,
cut into 4 squares
(available from Asian food shops)

75 g/3 oz white crab meat

75 g/3 oz smoked salmon, diced

25 g/1 oz shallots, finely chopped

¼ teaspoon chopped fresh dill

1 teaspoon white wine vinegar

2 teaspoons sesame oil

75 ml/2½ fl oz crème fraîche

a pinch of ground turmeric

salt and freshly ground
black pepper

FOR THE GARNISH:

a few leaves of frisée

4 fresh dill sprigs

4 fresh chervil sprigs

4 lamb's lettuce leaves

1 peeled, deseeded beef tomato

50 ml/1¾ fl oz soured cream

Press each piece of spring roll pastry into a 6 cm/ 2½ inch metal ring placed on a baking sheet, leaving the corners of the pastry overlapping the ring. Bake in an oven preheated to 200°C/400°F/Gas Mark 6 for about 5 minutes, until golden. Remove from the oven and leave to cool. Carefully remove the pastry from the rings and set aside.

Mix the crab meat, smoked salmon, shallots and dill together in a bowl. Whisk the vinegar and sesame oil together and add to the salmon mixture, then stir in the crème fraîche. Season with the turmeric and some salt and pepper.

Arrange the frisée, dill, chervil, lamb's lettuce and a slice of beef tomato on each serving plate. Fill the pastry moulds with the crab meat and smoked salmon mixture. Place next to the salad. Garnish the plate with a small spoonful of soured cream.

Pan-fried scallops served on tomato confit flavoured with black beans

Willi Elsener

ingredients

3 tablespoons vegetable oil

16 large fresh scallops, cleaned (no roe)

salt and freshly ground black pepper

FOR THE TOMATO CONFIT:

200 ml/7 fl oz olive oil

1 small shallot, finely chopped

50 ml/1¾ fl oz white wine vinegar

40 g/1½ oz caster sugar

100 ml/3½ fl oz tomato juice

½ garlic clove, finely chopped

½ teaspoon black bean sauce

300 g/10½ oz ripe cherry tomatoes, cut in half

½ teaspoon finely chopped fresh rosemary

½ teaspoon finely chopped fresh thyme

1 teaspoon finely chopped fresh coriander

1 teaspoon finely chopped fresh basil

FOR THE GARNISH:

4 gaufrette potato baskets (see Note opposite)

selection of salad leaves, such as lollo rosso, oakleaf, curly endive, lamb's lettuce, rocket

First make the confit. Heat the olive oil in a saucepan, add the shallot and sweat, without colouring, until translucent. Remove from the heat and add the vinegar, sugar, tomato juice, garlic and black bean sauce. Add the tomatoes and heat through gently without boiling. Season with salt and pepper, stir in the fresh herbs and set aside.

For the garnish, fill the potato baskets with the salad leaves and set aside.

Heat the vegetable oil in a non-stick frying pan. Season the scallops with salt and pepper, then put them in the pan over a high heat and brown on both sides. Reduce the heat and sauté for about 2 minutes, until cooked.

Meanwhile, put the tomato confit in 4 soup plates and place a potato basket in the centre of each plate. Arrange 4 scallops around each potato basket and then serve immediately.

NOTE

To make gaufrette potato baskets you will need a mandoline. Peel 2 large potatoes and slice them very thinly on the mandoline with the fluted blade, giving the potato a quarter turn after each slice to make a waffle pattern. Line a wire potato basket with overlapping slices of potato, clamp a smaller potato basket on top and deep-fry in hot oil until golden. Turn out and drain on kitchen paper. Repeat to make 4 baskets.

If you have difficulty obtaining wire potato baskets, you can clamp the slices of potato between two metal ladles, one slightly smaller than the other, then fry as above.

Oven-roasted quail breast with green mango and potato cake

ingredients

2 teaspoons honey

1 teaspoon finely chopped fresh ginger root

½ teaspoon garlic purée

60 ml/2 fl oz light soy sauce

4 boneless quail breasts

600 ml/1 pint good home-made quail, game or chicken stock

a little vegetable or olive oil for frying

100 g/4 oz mixed wild mushrooms

4 fresh rosemary sprigs

4 fresh thyme sprigs

salt and freshly ground black pepper

FOR THE GREEN MANGO AND POTATO CAKES:

1 tablespoon vegetable oil

100 g/4 oz green mango, peeled and shredded

50 g/2 oz courgette, shredded

50 g/2 oz butternut squash, peeled and shredded

50 g/2 oz potato, peeled and shredded

125 ml/4 fl oz double cream

4 egg yolks

freshly grated nutmeg

Mix together the honey, ginger, garlic and soy sauce and marinate the quail breasts in the mixture for about 1 hour.

Put the stock in a pan and boil until reduced in volume to about 150 ml/¼ pint, then set aside.

For the green mango and potato cakes, lightly brush four 6 cm/2½ inch non-stick straight-sided moulds with vegetable oil and line the bases with a circle of greaseproof paper (or you can use four lightly greased 6 cm/2½ inch baking rings – push a 7 cm/2¾ inch circle of greaseproof paper into the centre of each one so it comes slightly up the sides, then put them on a baking sheet). Heat the oil in a small pan, add the mango and shredded vegetables and sauté lightly until just tender, then transfer to a sieve and leave to cool. Press lightly to remove the liquid. Lightly whisk together the cream and egg yolks, season with nutmeg, salt and pepper and stir into the vegetables. Divide the mixture between the moulds and bake in an oven preheated to 160°C/325°F/ Gas Mark 3 for about 10–15 minutes, until golden brown and cooked through. Remove from the oven and leave to rest for 10 minutes. Carefully remove the cakes from the moulds and set aside.

To cook the quail, heat a little oil in a heavy-based frying pan, add the birds and brown briefly. Transfer to an oven preheated to 220°C/425°F/Gas Mark 7 and roast for about 8 minutes, until cooked through. Remove from the oven and keep warm.

For the sauce, sauté the wild mushrooms in a little oil until tender, then chop them roughly. Reheat the stock and stir in the mushrooms. Taste and add seasoning if necessary.

Pour the sauce on to each serving plate. Put a mango and potato cake in the centre and then place the quail on top of the cake. Garnish with the rosemary and thyme sprigs and serve.

Willi Elsener

Baked escalope of sea bass flavoured with lime and coriander and a port wine sauce

Willi Elsener

ingredients

4 teaspoons olive oil

½ teaspoon finely chopped
fresh coriander

a pinch of finely
grated lime zest

4 thick sea bass fillets, weighing
about 150 g/5 oz each

12 new potatoes, peeled and
part-cooked, ready for roasting

12 fresh shiitake mushrooms,
cut in half

12 pieces of Chinese flowering
cabbage, leaves removed, stalks
cooked and refreshed in cold water

12 small asparagus spears,
blanched and refreshed in
cold water

4 bay leaves, deep-fried,
to garnish

salt and freshly ground
black pepper

FOR THE SAUCE:

1 peeled shallot, finely sliced

200 ml/7 fl oz red wine

4 tablespoons port

200 ml/7 fl oz fish stock

4 tablespoons double cream

80 g/3 oz cold unsalted butter,
cut into cubes

Mix 1 teaspoon of the olive oil with the chopped coriander and lime zest. Slash the skin of each fish fillet several times to prevent it curling up when cooked. Now you need to form a pocket in each piece of fish to hold the coriander and lime mixture. To do this, put one piece in front of you skin-side down and, with a sharp knife, cut a slit along the edge on one side, about half way between the skin and the top surface. Cut in gently, leaving about 5 mm/¼ inch intact along the other 3 sides. Brush inside the pocket with the coriander and lime mixture. Repeat the process with the other pieces of fish. Set aside.

For the sauce, put the shallot, red wine, port and fish stock in a saucepan, bring to the boil and simmer until only 3 tablespoons of liquid remain. Add the cream and return to the boil, then pour the mixture through a sieve into a smaller pan, pressing out all the liquid. Return to the boil and remove from the heat. Very slowly whisk the butter cubes into the sauce. Season to taste. Keep the sauce warm but do not reheat or it will separate.

Heat a non-stick ovenproof frying pan, then pour in the remaining olive oil. Season the sea bass with salt and pepper and place skin-side down in the pan. Brown, then turn the pieces over and transfer to an oven preheated to 200°C/400°F/Gas Mark 6. Bake for about 8 minutes or until just cooked. Remove the fish from the pan and keep warm.

Add the potatoes to the pan, return to the oven and cook for 3 – 4 minutes. Add the mushrooms. When the mushrooms are cooked, add the Chinese cabbage stalks and asparagus to the pan to warm through. Season with salt and pepper.

Arrange the roast potatoes, mushrooms, Chinese cabbage stalks and asparagus in the centre of 4 serving plates and place the sea bass on top. Place a deep-fried bay leaf vertically in the centre of each piece of fish. Pour the sauce around and serve.

Apple and cinnamon cake served with Calvados ice cream

Willi Elsener

ingredients

1 tablespoon brandy

40 g/1½ oz currants

125 g/4½ oz self-raising flour

½ teaspoon salt

60 g/2¼ oz butter

60 g/2¼ oz caster sugar

½ teaspoon ground ginger

¼ teaspoon ground cinnamon

225 g/8 oz apples (Discovery or Golden Delicious, if possible)

1 medium egg, lightly beaten

chocolate sauce and crème anglaise or cream, to serve (optional)

raspberries and fresh mint sprigs, to decorate (optional)

icing sugar, to decorate (optional)

FOR THE CALVADOS ICE CREAM:

5 egg yolks

125 g/4½ oz caster sugar

500 ml/17 fl oz milk

150 ml/¼ pint whipping cream

1 tablespoon Calvados

First make the ice cream: beat the egg yolks and sugar together in a bowl until slightly foamy. Heat the milk almost to boiling point, then gradually pour it on to the egg yolk mixture, beating constantly. Pour the mixture back into the saucepan and cook over a low heat, stirring constantly, until it is thick enough to coat the back of the spoon. Do not let it boil or it will curdle. Remove from the heat and stir vigorously until cool, then strain through a fine sieve. Stir in the cream and Calvados.

Freeze the mixture in an ice-cream machine until firm. If you don't have an ice-cream machine, pour it into a shallow bowl, cover and freeze for 2 hours, until it begins to firm up. Transfer the half-frozen ice cream to a blender or food processor and whizz until it is creamy and the ice crystals have broken down. Pour back into the bowl, cover and return to the freezer. Freeze until it firms up again, then whizz in the blender or food processor as before. Cover and freeze again, whizzing one more time, then freeze until firm.

For the cake, butter four 10 cm/4 inch fluted flan tins, line the base of each one with a circle of greased greaseproof paper and dust lightly with flour. Pour the brandy over the currants and set aside.

Sift the self-raising flour and salt into a bowl and rub in the butter. Stir in the sugar, ginger and cinnamon. Peel the apples, then cut them into quarters and remove the core with a knife. Cut the apples crossways into slices 3 mm/⅛ inch thick, then add to the mixture. Add the soaked currants and the egg and mix thoroughly. Spoon the mixture into the prepared tins and smooth the top.

Bake for 20–25 minutes in an oven preheated to 180°C/350°F/Gas Mark 4. The cakes are done when a skewer inserted into the centre comes out clean. Remove from the oven and leave in the tins for about 10 minutes, then turn out. Serve with the Calvados ice cream. You could also drizzle with chocolate sauce and crème anglaise or cream, if desired, and decorate with raspberries and mint sprigs. If using the icing sugar, dust lightly and serve.

Valentina Harris was born and brought up in Rome, the youngest of a large Anglo-Italian family. She moved to the UK in 1976 and published her first book, *Perfect Pasta*, in 1984. Subsequent books include *Italian Regional Cookery*, which accompanied her 1990 BBC television series, *Valentina's Complete Italian Cookery Course*, *Italian Family Feast*, and *Southern Italian Cooking*.

A qualified cookery teacher, Valentina gives classes and demonstrations both in the UK and in countries as diverse as South Africa, Japan, New Zealand and Australia. She appears regularly on radio and contributes to numerous publications, including *The Times*, the *Evening Standard* and *Homes and Gardens*. She also appears on the BBC's popular 'Ready Steady Cook' programme.

Valentina Harris

Valentina Harris

cooks at
Hampton Court Palace

"I decided to produce a true Italian feast – lots of food steeped in flavour."

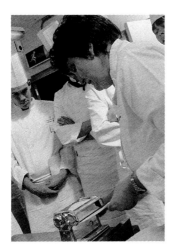

menu
serves 6

Appetizers
Crisp ravioli with a sole filling
Crisp tortellini in the Bolognese style
Deep-fried sage leaves

Warm seafood salad of the Adriatic

Rolled pasta filled with
  ricotta and spinach

Lamb cutlets with prosciutto
  and mozzarella
Roast potatoes with lemon
  and rosemary
Artichokes braised in the
  Roman style

Watermelon sorbet

wine suggestions

Albizzia Bianco di Toscana
  Frescobaldi 1993

Remole Chianti Frescobaldi 1993

Montesodi, Chianti Rufina,
  Frescobaldi 1990

Moscato di Pantelleria and Passito
  di Pantelleria Pellegrino

Crisp ravioli with a sole filling

Valentina Harris

ingredients

1½ tablespoons olive oil

2 canned anchovy fillets, drained, soaked in milk for 30 minutes, then rinsed and dried

½ onion, finely chopped

1 celery stick, finely chopped

½ carrot, finely chopped

1 garlic clove, finely chopped

1½ tablespoons chopped fresh flat-leaf parsley, plus extra to garnish

2 tablespoons tomato purée, diluted in 1½ tablespoons hot water

175 g/6 oz sole fillet, coarsely chopped

sunflower oil for deep-frying

sea salt and freshly ground black pepper

FOR THE PASTA DOUGH:

500 g/1 lb 2 oz plain white flour (preferably Italian '00' flour)

5 eggs

salt

Heat the olive oil in a saucepan with the anchovy fillets. Mash the anchovies to a pulp, then add the onion, celery, carrot, garlic and parsley. Mix together and fry gently for about 10 minutes or until soft. Add the tomato purée and simmer for about 15 minutes. Add the fish. Mix again and cook for 5–10 minutes, until a thick sauce has formed and the fish has broken up. Season to taste, then leave to cool completely.

To make the pasta dough, pile the flour on to a work surface and plunge your fist into the centre to make a hollow. Break the eggs into the hollow and add a small pinch of salt. With your fingers, beat the eggs roughly into the flour, then use both your hands to knead everything together thoroughly until you have a smooth, pliable ball of dough – this should take about 10 minutes. Wrap half the dough in clingfilm and refrigerate for making Crisp tortellini in the Bolognese style (see opposite). Divide the remaining dough into 3 or 4 pieces and roll out as thinly as possible, using a pasta machine or a rolling pin.

As you make the ravioli, you'll need to work fast to prevent the sheets of dough drying out. Work out your best method: either roll out the dough a little at a time and cover it with damp cloths or divide the work amongst friends! The dough should be kept pliable at all times, so don't leave it sitting on the table.

Dot teaspoonfuls of the filling along the sheet, about 4 cm/1½ inches apart, in evenly spaced rows. Lay a second sheet of dough on top and press around each covered mound of filling with the sides of your hands to press out all the air. Cut around each mound with a ravioli cutter or pastry cutter. They can be square or round, or even triangular.

Heat the sunflower oil until sizzling hot. Fry the ravioli in batches until crisp, golden and slightly puffy. Scoop them out of the hot oil, drain thoroughly on kitchen paper and then arrange them on platters, sprinkle with sea salt and chopped fresh flat-leaf parsley and serve.

Crisp tortellini in the Bolognese style

ingredients

15 g/½ oz unsalted butter

50 g/2 oz pork loin, diced

25 g/1 oz trimmed veal loin, diced

25 g/1 oz mortadella, diced

50 g/2 oz turkey breast, diced

25 g/1 oz prosciutto crudo, diced

1 egg yolk

100 g/4 oz Parmesan cheese, freshly grated

a pinch of freshly grated nutmeg

½ quantity of Pasta dough (see Crisp ravioli with a sole filling, opposite)

sunflower oil for deep-frying

sea salt and freshly ground black pepper

Melt the butter in a saucepan, add all the meat and cook slowly for about 10 minutes, stirring frequently to brown it all over. Remove from the heat and chop or process to a fine texture. Add the egg yolk and half the Parmesan. Season to taste with nutmeg, salt and pepper. Stir thoroughly until everything is well combined, then set aside until required.

Roll out the pasta dough as for the ravioli. Cut it into 5 cm/2 inch squares. Put a tiny amount of filling in the centre of each square and fold in half to make a triangle. Wrap the 2 outside corners of the triangle around your index finger and press them together. Fold the third, upturned corner down and backwards, then slip the tortellino off the end of your finger.

When they are all formed and looking like belly buttons in neat rows, heat the oil until sizzling hot. Fry the tortellini in batches until crisp, golden and slightly puffy. Scoop them out of the hot oil, drain thoroughly on kitchen paper and then arrange them on platters, sprinkled with the remaining Parmesan to serve.

Valentina Harris

Deep-fried sage leaves

ingredients

130 fresh sage leaves, washed and dried

2 tablespoons anchovy paste

40 g/1½ oz plain flour

1 egg white

150 ml/¼ pint olive oil (not extra virgin)

salt

Sandwich together pairs of sage leaves with a little anchovy paste. Beat the flour with about 5–6 tablespoons of water to make a batter the consistency of double cream. Season to taste with salt. Beat the egg white until stiff, then fold it into the batter. Dip the leaf sandwiches into the batter to coat them.

Heat the oil in a small, deep pan until sizzling and fry the sage leaves for a few minutes, until golden and crisp. Drain on kitchen paper and serve very hot.

Warm seafood salad of the Adriatic

Valentina Harris

ingredients

30 fresh mussels, cleaned

60 fresh baby clams, cleaned

1 large bay leaf

1½ lemons

300 g/10½ oz cleaned fresh squid, cut into neat strips and rings

250 g/9 oz small raw prawns

6 large raw Mediterranean prawns

140 ml/4½ fl oz extra virgin olive oil

5 tablespoons chopped fresh flat-leaf parsley

sea salt and freshly ground black pepper

salad leaves and lemon slices, to serve

Steam the mussels and clams with the bay leaf and half a lemon for about 8 minutes, until the shells open. Discard any that remained closed. Steam the squid briefly until opaque. Steam the small and large prawns until they turn pink, then leave to cool almost completely before shelling. Remove the mussels from their shells (don't shell the clams) and put them in a large warmed bowl with the clams, prawns and squid. Mix them all together. Squeeze the juice from the remaining lemon and add it to the seafood with the oil, parsley and pepper to taste. Season with salt after mixing. Serve tepid, piled on to salad leaves and garnished with lemon slices.

Rolled pasta filled with ricotta and spinach

ingredients

500 g/1lb 2 oz fresh spinach

200 g/7 oz extremely fresh ricotta cheese

150 g/5 oz Parmesan cheese, freshly grated

2 eggs, beaten

a pinch of freshly grated nutmeg

1 quantity of Pasta dough (see page 46)

sea salt and freshly ground black pepper

For the tomato sauce, put all the ingredients into a saucepan. Cover and bring to the boil, then simmer for 30 minutes. Remove the lid and continue to simmer for about 20 minutes, until most of the liquid has evaporated. Remove from the heat and push through a food mill or sieve. Season to taste with salt.

Wash the spinach well, then cook it in just the water clinging to its leaves. Drain thoroughly and chop finely. Mix with the ricotta, Parmesan, eggs and nutmeg. Season to taste and stir vigorously until smooth.

FOR THE TOMATO SAUCE:

1 kg/2¼ lb ripe tomatoes, skinned and quartered, or canned tomatoes, drained and quartered

1 small onion, quartered

1 carrot, quartered

1 celery stick, quartered

1 large fresh parsley sprig

7 fresh basil leaves

3 tablespoons extra virgin olive oil

Roll the pasta out very thinly by hand into a wide sheet. Spread the filling over it, leaving a 4 cm/1½ inch border, and then roll the pasta up like a swiss roll, making sure there is no air between each turn of the spiral. Wrap it tightly in a clean muslin cloth. Tie the ends securely.

Bring a fish kettle of salted water to the boil. Slide the wrapped roll into the water carefully (don't let it sag in the centre) and simmer for about 30 minutes. Remove carefully and drain. Unwrap and lay on a board, then slice with a very sharp knife. Reheat the tomato sauce if necessary. Serve the pasta slices with the tomato sauce.

Lamb cutlets with prosciutto and mozzarella

ingredients

12 lamb cutlets

3 tablespoons plain flour

2 eggs, beaten

5 tablespoons dried white breadcrumbs

6 tablespoons olive oil (not extra virgin)

100 g/4 oz prosciutto crudo, very thinly sliced

150 g/5 oz mozzarella cheese, cut into 12 slices

sea salt and freshly ground black pepper

Trim the cutlets carefully and flatten them as much as possible with a meat mallet. Coat them lightly in the flour, then dip in the beaten egg and finally coat in the breadcrumbs.

Heat the oil in a frying pan until sizzling, then fry the lamb cutlets on each side until golden brown and crisp. Remove from the pan, drain thoroughly on kitchen paper and season to taste. Arrange the cutlets on a baking tray, lay a slice of ham and a slice of Mozzarella on each one and bake in an oven preheated to 220°C/425°F/Gas Mark 7 for 5 minutes, until the cheese begins to run. Transfer to a serving platter and serve at once.

Valentina Harris

Roast potatoes with lemon and rosemary

ingredients

6 medium-sized yellow-fleshed potatoes

1½ lemons, sliced

1½ tablespoons fresh rosemary leaves

140 ml/4½ fl oz extra virgin olive oil

175 ml/6 fl oz water

sea salt and freshly ground black pepper

Wash the potatoes but do not peel them. Cut them into fat, long chunks and place in a large shallow roasting tin. Add the lemon slices and rosemary. Toss well, add the oil and water and toss again.

Bake in an oven preheated to 200°C/400°F/Gas Mark 6. Usually the potatoes are cooked after 1–1½ hours. Remember to toss them a couple of times while cooking and to add extra water or oil if they look as if they are drying out.

Artichokes braised in the Roman style

ingredients

12 Italian globe artichokes

1 lemon

6 garlic cloves, thinly sliced

a small handful of fresh mint leaves, chopped

2 tumblers of cold water

½ tumbler of extra virgin olive oil

sea salt and freshly ground black pepper

Remove all the hard outer leaves from the artichokes until only the tender, pale-green leaves are left. Cut off the sharp points of the remaining leaves. Trim the stalks and peel them. Pull open the inner leaves and scoop out the hairy choke. Pull the artichokes apart so that they look like open flowers. Rub them all over with half the lemon as you prepare them and drop them into a bowl of water in which the remaining lemon half has been squeezed and is left floating. This will prevent oxidization.

When you are ready to cook, drain and dry the artichokes, then insert a few slices of garlic into each one. Sprinkle the insides with salt and pepper and divide the mint leaves evenly between the artichokes. Place them upright in an ovenproof dish, pour the water around and over them and sprinkle with a little more salt. Pour the oil on and around the artichokes, then cover and bake in an oven preheated to 190°C/375°F/ Gas Mark 5 for about 40 minutes, basting frequently. Serve hot or cold.

Valentina Harris

Watermelon sorbet

Push the watermelon through a sieve and mix it thoroughly with half the sugar and the jasmine or orange flower water. Pour it into a mould and freeze until slushy, stirring every 10 minutes or so to break up the ice crystals. When it is thick and slushy, stir in the chocolate, the remaining sugar, the nuts, candied pumpkin or pear and cinnamon. Return to the freezer and freeze until solid, stirring occasionally.

When you are ready to serve, dip the mould into hot water to loosen the edges, then turn the sorbet out on to a platter. Serve with Italian biscuits, if liked.

ingredients

500 g/1 lb 2 oz watermelon flesh (no seeds or skin)

300 g/10½ oz caster sugar

2 tablespoons jasmine flower water or 2 teaspoons orange flower water

100 g/4 oz good-quality plain chocolate, finely diced

40 g/1½ oz pistachio nuts, chopped

100 g/4 oz candied pumpkin or pear, chopped (available from Italian delicatessens)

1 teaspoon ground cinnamon

Italian biscuits, to serve (optional)

Valentina Harris

Born and brought up in Bolton, Paul Heathcote trained under Francis Coulson at the legendary Lake District hotel Sharrow Bay, and later worked at Le Manoir aux Quat' Saisons under Raymond Blanc, whom he describes as his greatest influence. In 1990 Paul realized a long-held ambition with the establishment of his eponymous restaurant in Longridge, near Preston. In 1994 it was awarded two Michelin stars and he has received many plaudits for his *haute cuisine* restyling of British cooking. In 1994 he won the Egon Ronay Chef of the Year Award, then a second CATEY award in 1997 for Restaurateur of the Year. Recently he opened Heathcote's Brasserie in Preston and Simply Heathcote's in Manchester. November 1997 saw the opening of his chefs' training centre, 'Heathcote's School of Excellence'.

Paul
Heathcote

Paul Heathcote
cooks at
Blackburn Rovers

"This menu features some of my favourite dishes. I was keen for the chefs to understand the importance of developing the flavours of the food."

menu

serves 4

Heathcote's black pudding with
crushed potatoes, baked beans
and bay leaf sauce

Roast cod with warm 'potted
shrimps', red wine sauce and
deep-fried parsley

Goosnargh duckling with cider
potatoes and caramelized onions

Bread and butter pudding with
apricot compote and clotted cream

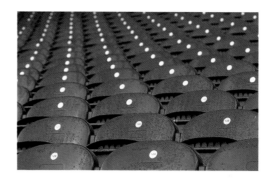

wine suggestions

Kendall-Jackson Zinfandel, Gold
Coast Vineyards 1992/3

Meursault, Louis Jadot 1993/4

Gevrey-Chambertin, Louis Jadot 1987

Monbazillac, Château la Gironic,
G Pelletant 1993

Heathcote's black pudding with crushed potatoes, baked beans and bay leaf sauce

Paul Heathcote

ingredients

50 g/2 oz sultanas

3 bay leaves, crushed

125 ml/4 fl oz white wine vinegar

500 g/1 lb 2 oz veal or
lamb's sweetbreads

olive oil

500 ml/17 fl oz pig's blood

¼ onion, chopped and boiled
until soft

50 g/2 oz rolled oats

leaves from 1 fresh rosemary sprig

leaves from 1 fresh thyme sprig

1 black pudding skin, 45 cm/
18 inches long

300 ml/½ pint veal stock

2 large potatoes

100 g/4 oz unsalted butter, diced

8–12 button onions, cooked

50 g/2 oz white haricot
beans, cooked

50 g/2 oz carrot, diced and cooked

salt and freshly ground
black pepper

Place the sultanas in a bowl with 1 bay leaf, add the vinegar and soak until the sultanas are plump and swollen. Transfer to a small pan, bring to the boil and simmer gently until most of the vinegar has evaporated (do not allow it to caramelize). Remove the bay leaf.

Blanch the sweetbreads in boiling water for 1 minute, then lift them out and peel off the outside membrane. Cut into large dice. Heat a little olive oil in a pan, add the sweetbreads and fry until golden brown. Set aside.

Place the pig's blood in a warm bain-marie and stir occasionally until it starts to thicken. Pass through a sieve to remove any membrane. Gently mix the blood with the sweetbreads, sultanas, boiled chopped onion and rolled oats. Add the rosemary, thyme and some seasoning, then carefully fill the black pudding skin. Poach the pudding in a bain-marie at just below boiling point (about 82°C/180°F) until the pudding has reached 75°C/165°F in the centre when tested with a thermometer. Leave to cool, then slice off 4 portions and set aside.

To make the sauce, bring the veal stock to the boil with the remaining bay leaves and simmer gently until reduced to a coating consistency. Remove the bay leaves and check the seasoning.

To make the crushed potatoes, boil them in their skins until cooked but still slightly firm, then peel while still hot. Mash the diced butter with a fork and lightly crush with the potatoes. Season to taste.

To serve, brush the 4 portions of black pudding with olive oil and place under a hot grill for about 4–5 minutes, until heated through. Add the cooked button onions, haricot beans and diced carrot to the sauce and reheat. Place a mound of crushed potatoes on each of 4 heated dinner plates or in shallow soup bowls and arrange the slices of black pudding on top, then pour the sauce over and around the pudding.

Roast cod with warm 'potted shrimps', red wine sauce and deep-fried parsley

Paul Heathcote

ingredients

350 g/12 oz cod fillet, skin on

rock salt

oil for frying

salt and freshly ground black pepper

FOR THE RED WINE SAUCE:

6 shallots, chopped

2 garlic cloves, chopped

oil for frying

4 star anise

grated zest of 1 orange

1 fresh thyme sprig

250 ml/8 fl oz red wine

250 ml/8 fl oz fish stock

125 ml/4 fl oz veal stock

a pinch of sugar (optional)

FOR THE WARM 'POTTED SHRIMPS':

a small knob of butter

1 shallot, finely chopped

1 tablespoon white wine vinegar

3 tablespoons white wine

a drop of cream

75 g/3 oz butter, chilled and diced

cayenne pepper

lemon juice

125 g/4½ oz brown shrimps

25 g/1 oz chopped fresh flat-leaf parsley

FOR THE DEEP-FRIED PARSLEY:

vegetable oil for deep-frying

8 large fresh curly parsley sprigs

Remove all the scales from the cod with the back of a knife, then take out any pin bones with pliers or tweezers. Wash the fish in cold water and pat dry. Score the skin with a sharp knife and place skin-side down on some rock salt. Leave for 1 hour. Wipe off excess salt and cut the cod into 4 pieces. Set aside.

For the red wine sauce, brown the shallots and garlic in a splash of oil in a heavy-based pan. Add the star anise and orange zest and cook, stirring, for about 1 minute. Add the thyme and red wine and boil until the liquid is reduced by half. Add the fish stock and veal stock and boil until reduced by one third. Pass through a fine sieve, then season to taste, adding the sugar if necessary. Keep warm.

For the shrimps, heat the butter in a small pan, add the shallot and sweat until tender. Add the vinegar and wine and boil until reduced by about four fifths. Stir in the cream and then whisk in the cold butter a few pieces at a time. Season with cayenne pepper, lemon juice, salt and pepper. Stir in the brown shrimps and chopped parsley. Keep warm.

Heat a little oil in a heavy-based pan, add the cod, skin-side down, and cook until golden and crisp, then turn to cook the other side.

Meanwhile, heat some oil for deep-frying, drop in the parsley sprigs 2 or 3 at a time and cook for a few seconds, until bright green and frizzled. Drain the sprigs on kitchen paper.

To serve, place the shrimps in the centre of 4 warmed serving plates and place the cod on top. Pour the red wine sauce around and top the cod with the deep-fried parsley sprigs.

Goosnargh duckling with cider potatoes and caramelized onions

ingredients

4 duck breasts

1 small Savoy cabbage, shredded

100 g/4 oz peas

500 ml/17 fl oz well-flavoured duck stock

salt and freshly ground black pepper

FOR THE CARAMELIZED ONIONS:

oil for frying

20 button onions, peeled

50 g/2 oz granulated sugar

FOR THE CIDER POTATOES:

4 large, even-sized potatoes, peeled and cut into even rounds about 2 cm/¾ inch thick

125 ml/4 fl oz sweet cider

250 g/9 oz clarified unsalted butter (see page 146)

For the onions, heat a thin layer of oil in a pan large enough to hold the onions in a single layer. Add them and sauté for a few minutes. Sprinkle in the sugar and cook until the onions are caramelized all over. Pour in enough water to cover. Simmer until the onions are tender and the water has evaporated. Season and keep warm.

For the potatoes, pour the cider into a pan large enough to hold them in a single layer (reserve a little cider for the sauce), add the butter and simmer gently until the potatoes are cooked and golden. Turn up the heat towards the end if necessary to colour the potatoes. Season well.

Roast the duck breasts in an oven preheated to 200°C/400°F/Gas Mark 6 for 12–15 minutes, until pink. Meanwhile, cook the cabbage and peas in separate pans of lightly salted water until tender, then drain. Bring the stock to the boil with the reserved cider, then season and set aside. Remove the duck breasts from the bone and place under a hot grill until the skin is crisp.

To serve, place the potatoes and cabbage on 4 plates. Slice the duck and arrange on top. Scatter over the peas and onions, then pour over the cider-scented stock.

Paul Heathcote

Bread and butter pudding with apricot compote and clotted cream

Paul Heathcote

ingredients

3 eggs

50 g/2 oz caster sugar

225 ml/7½ fl oz milk

225 ml/7½ fl oz whipping cream

1 vanilla pod

75 g/3 oz butter

5 thin slices of white bread

75 g/3 oz sultanas

25 g/1 oz icing sugar

50 g/2 oz apricot jam, melted
with a little water

clotted cream, to serve

FOR THE APRICOT COMPOTE:

250 g/9 oz dried apricots

250 ml/8 fl oz boiling water

½ vanilla pod, split open

grated zest of ½ orange

½ cinnamon stick

First make the apricot compote: put the apricots in a pan and pour the boiling water over them. Leave to stand for about 30 minutes, then add the remaining ingredients, bring to the boil and simmer for about 10 minutes. Leave to cool.

Whisk the eggs and sugar together, then whisk in the milk and cream. Strain through a fine sieve. Slit open the vanilla pod and scrape the seeds out into the egg mixture. Mix well.

Butter the bread, remove the crusts and cut each piece into quarters. Arrange a layer of bread in a greased ovenproof dish and sprinkle over the sultanas. Arrange the rest of the bread on top. Pour the vanilla custard mixture over the bread and leave to soak for 5 minutes.

Place the dish in a bain-marie and bake in an oven preheated to 160°C/325°F/Gas Mark 3 for about 30 minutes or until the custard is set. Cool slightly, then dust with the icing sugar and glaze under a hot grill until golden. Brush with the melted apricot jam, then serve with the apricot compote and clotted cream.

Ken Hom was born in America and has travelled the globe as a food and restaurant consultant, conducting cookery demonstrations and appearing on radio and television shows. He has worked with some of the world's most famous hotels, including the Oriental in Bangkok and the Regent in Sydney, and is a regular contributor to *The Financial Times* and the *New York Times*.

An acknowledged authority on Chinese cuisine, he has won a devoted audience for his BBC television series, 'Ken Hom's Chinese Cookery', 'Ken Hom's Hot Wok', 'Travels with a Hot Wok' and 'Hot Chefs'. He is the author of the bestselling books of the same name, plus *East Meets West Cuisine* and *Illustrated Chinese Cookery*.

Ken Hom

Ken Hom
cooks at
Lords Cricket Ground

"Lords provided a unique backdrop for my menu. I wanted the food to be fun to prepare and finished just at the last minute before serving."

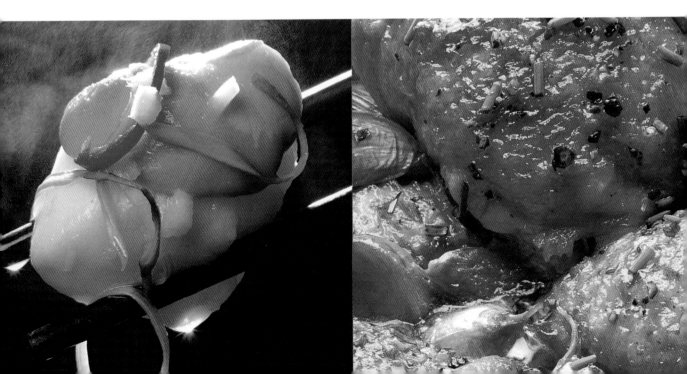

menu 1

serves 4

Steamed scallops with chilli
and ginger

Slow-braised chicken with
whole garlic
Garlic fried rice
Hot beanthread noodles with
vegetables, beancurd and spices
Spicy stir-fried broccoli

Poached pears with ginger scented
with vanilla and lemon

wine suggestions

Fetzer Barrel Select Chardonnay -
Californian North Coast

Château Moulin Riche St Julien 1990

Museum Show Reserve Ruther
Glen Muscat

Steamed scallops
with chilli and ginger

Perhaps the best way to preserve the qualities of fresh scallops is the Chinese technique of steaming. Their briny seafood taste is emphasized and the bonus is that they are very simple to prepare and take literally minutes to cook.

Arrange the scallops on a heatproof platter. Then evenly distribute all the remaining ingredients on top.

Next set up a steamer or put a rack into a wok or deep pan and fill it with 5 cm/2 inches of water. Bring the water to the boil over a high heat. Carefully lower the platter of scallops into the steamer or on to the rack. Turn the heat to low and cover the wok or pan tightly. Steam gently for 5 minutes. Remove and serve at once.

ingredients

450 g/1 lb fresh scallops, including the corals

2 fresh red chillies, deseeded and chopped

2 teaspoons finely chopped fresh ginger root

1 tablespoon Shaoxing rice wine or dry sherry

1 tablespoon light soy sauce

¼ teaspoon salt

¼ teaspoon freshly ground black pepper

3 tablespoons shredded spring onions

Slow-braised chicken with whole garlic

ingredients

900 g/2 lb chicken thighs, with bone in

2 teaspoons salt

1 teaspoon freshly ground black pepper

2 tablespoons plain flour

3 tablespoons groundnut oil

15 whole garlic cloves, unpeeled

2 tablespoons Shaoxing rice wine or dry sherry

1 tablespoon light soy sauce

3 tablespoons chicken stock or water

2 tablespoons finely snipped fresh chives

Blot the chicken thighs dry with kitchen paper. Sprinkle them evenly with the salt and pepper, then sprinkle with the flour, shaking off any excess.

Heat a wok or large frying pan over a high heat until it is hot. Add the oil and, when it is very hot and slightly smoking, turn the heat to low. Add the chicken skin-side down and brown slowly on both sides for about 10 minutes. Drain off all the excess fat, add the garlic and stir-fry for 2 minutes. Then add the Shaoxing rice wine or dry sherry, soy sauce and stock or water. Turn the heat to as low as possible, cover and braise for 20 minutes, until the chicken is tender.

When the chicken and garlic are cooked, remove them from the wok with a slotted spoon and place them on a warm platter. Sprinkle with the chives and serve at once.

Garlic fried rice

ingredients

enough long-grain white rice to fill a measuring jug to the 400 ml/14 fl oz level

600 ml/1 pint water

2 tablespoons groundnut oil

225 g/8 oz onions, coarsely chopped

3 tablespoons coarsely chopped garlic

2 teaspoons salt

½ teaspoon freshly ground black pepper

2 tablespoons finely chopped fresh coriander

Prepare the rice at least 2 hours in advance: put it in a large bowl and wash in several changes of water until the water becomes clear. Drain the rice, put it in a pan with the water and bring to the boil. Boil for 15 minutes or until most of the surface liquid has evaporated and the surface of the rice has small indentations like pitted craters. Cover with a very tight-fitting lid, turn the heat down as low as possible and let the rice cook undisturbed for 15 minutes. Leave to cool completely and then put it in the fridge.

Just before serving the rice, heat a wok or large frying pan over a high heat until it is hot. Add the oil and, when it is very hot and slightly smoking, add the onions, garlic, salt and pepper. Stir-fry for 4 minutes. Then add the rice and continue to stir-fry for 5 minutes or until it is heated through. Finally add the fresh coriander. Give the mixture several good stirs. Turn on to a warm platter and serve.

Hot beanthread noodles with vegetables, beancurd and spices

ingredients

175 g/6 oz beanthread (transparent) noodles

1 tablespoon groundnut oil

2 tablespoons salted black beans, coarsely chopped

3 tablespoons finely chopped spring onions, plus 2 teaspoons to garnish

2 tablespoons coarsely chopped garlic

1 tablespoon finely chopped fresh ginger root

100 g/4 oz carrots, finely shredded

100 g/4 oz firm fresh beancurd, drained on kitchen paper and shredded

225 g/8 oz Chinese flowering cabbage or bok choy, finely shredded

300 ml/½ pint water

2 tablespoons Shaoxing rice wine or dry sherry

1½ tablespoons chilli bean sauce

1 tablespoon whole yellow bean sauce

2 tablespoons light soy sauce

2 teaspoons dark soy sauce

½ teaspoon salt

½ teaspoon freshly ground black pepper

2 teaspoons sesame oil

Soak the noodles in a large bowl of warm water for 15 minutes. When they are soft, drain them and discard the water. Cut them into 7.5 cm/3 inch lengths, using scissors or a knife.

Heat a wok or large frying pan over a high heat until it is hot. Add the oil and, when it is very hot and slightly smoking, add the black beans, spring onions, garlic and ginger and stir-fry quickly for 15 seconds. Add the carrots and stir-fry for 2 minutes, then add the beancurd and cabbage. Carefully mix together without breaking up the beancurd. Then add all the rest of the ingredients except the sesame oil and noodles and cook the mixture over a gentle heat for about 2 minutes. Now add the drained noodles and sesame oil and cook the mixture for a further 3 minutes.

Ladle some noodles into individual bowls or one large serving bowl, garnish with the remaining spring onions and serve at once.

Spicy stir-fried broccoli

ingredients

450 g/1 lb broccoli

1½ tablespoons groundnut oil

2 tablespoons coarsely chopped garlic

1 teaspoon salt

½ teaspoon freshly ground black pepper

2 tablespoons Shaoxing rice wine or dry sherry

1 tablespoon chilli bean sauce

1 teaspoon sugar

4–5 tablespoons water

2 teaspoons sesame oil

Separate the broccoli heads into small florets and peel and slice the stems. Blanch the broccoli pieces in a large pan of boiling salted water until just tender, then immerse them in cold water. Drain thoroughly.

Heat a wok or large frying pan over a high heat until it is hot. Add the oil and, when it is very hot and slightly smoking, add the garlic, salt, pepper, rice wine or dry sherry, chilli bean sauce and sugar. Stir-fry for a few seconds, then add the blanched broccoli and the water. Stir-fry over a moderate to high heat for 4 minutes, until the broccoli is thoroughly heated through. Add the sesame oil and continue to stir-fry for 30 seconds. The broccoli is now ready to serve.

Poached pears with ginger scented with vanilla and lemon

If using a wok to make this dessert, make sure it is a non-reactive one – that is, a non-stick wok. A basic carbon steel wok will react to the acid from the lemon and may lose its seasoning.

ingredients

4 firm pears

juice of 1 lemon

6 tablespoons Chinese rock sugar or granulated sugar

600 ml/1 pint water

1 vanilla pod, split in half lengthways

8 slices of fresh ginger root

long strips of lemon zest, to decorate

Peel the pears, sprinkle with the lemon juice and set them aside.

Combine the sugar, water, vanilla pod and fresh ginger in a non-stick wok or pan and boil until the sugar has completely dissolved. Add the pears, cover and simmer over a low heat for 20–25 minutes or until they are tender. The cooking time will depend on the ripeness of the pears.

When the pears are cooked, remove them with a slotted spoon, together with the vanilla pod and ginger slices. Over a high heat, reduce the liquid to a syrup by boiling it fast. Discard the ginger slices but keep the vanilla pod and, when it dries, put it in sugar to keep for future use.

Pour the syrup over the pears, decorate with lemon zest and serve at once, with cream or ice cream, if liked. Alternatively, you can leave the pears to cool, cover them with clingfilm and chill until ready to serve.

Ken Hom
cooks at Kenley House

"I chose, on this occasion, to present a more 'fusion'-influenced menu."

menu 2

serves 4

Fried cucumber stuffed
  with spicy pork

Crackling rice-paper-wrapped sea
  bass served with infused oils

Stir-fried chicken with chargrilled
  sweet peppers

Warmed berry compote with basil

wine suggestions

Dopff Gewürztraminer Moulin Blanc 1995

Byron Pinot Noir 1994

Petaluma Riesling 1995

Muscat de Rivesaltes Chapoutier 1996

Fried cucumber stuffed with spicy pork

ingredients

700 g/1½ lb cucumbers

2 tablespoons cornflour

3 tablespoons groundnut oil

fresh coriander sprigs, to garnish

FOR THE STUFFING:

225 g/8 oz fatty pork, finely minced

1 egg white

1½ tablespoons finely chopped
spring onions

2 teaspoons Shaoxing rice
wine or dry sherry

2 teaspoons light soy sauce

2 teaspoons sugar

1 teaspoon salt

1 teaspoon freshly ground
black pepper

1 teaspoon seasoning oil

FOR THE SAUCE

300 ml/½ pint chicken stock

2 tablespoons Shaoxing rice
wine or dry sherry

2 tablespoons light soy sauce

1 tablespoon oyster sauce

2 teaspoons sugar

1 teaspoon cornflour blended
with 2 teaspoons water

2 teaspoons sesame oil

2 tablespoons finely chopped
fresh coriander

Cut the cucumbers into slices 2.5 cm/1 inch thick but don't peel them. Remove the seeds and pulp from the centre of each cucumber slice, using a small sharp knife. Hollow the cucumber so that you have at least a 5 mm/¼ inch shell. Lightly dust the hollow interior of the cucumber slices with the cornflour. Mix all the stuffing ingredients together in a large bowl. Then stuff each cucumber ring with this mixture.

Heat a wok or large frying pan and add the groundnut oil. When it is moderately hot, add some of the stuffed cucumber rings and cook them slowly until they are slightly browned underneath. Turn them over and brown the other side (you may have to brown them in several batches, adding more oil if necessary). Remove the cucumber rings from the oil with a slotted spoon and put them on a plate. When you have fried all the cucumber rings, wipe the wok or pan clean.

Reheat the wok or pan, add all the sauce ingredients except the sesame oil and coriander and bring to a simmer. Add the stuffed cucumber rings. Cover the pan with a lid and simmer slowly for 7 minutes or until the cucumber is completely cooked. Transfer the rings to a warm serving platter, lifting them out of the sauce with a slotted spoon. Boil the sauce over a high heat until reduced in volume by a third. Then stir in the sesame oil and fresh coriander. Pour the sauce over the stuffed cucumber and serve at once, garnished with coriander.

Crackling rice-paper-wrapped sea bass served with infused oils

This surprisingly easy dish is a typical example of fusion cooking. It uses rice paper (an Asian ingredient) to wrap sea bass (a very European fish), seasoned with Asian and Western herbs and a touch of Madras curry powder. You can use halibut or cod instead of sea bass.

ingredients

450 g/1 lb skinned sea bass fillet

1 teaspoon salt

½ teaspoon freshly ground five-pepper mixture (available from Chinese food shops and some supermarkets)

2 teaspoons Madras curry powder

2 tablespoons plain flour

2 tablespoons water

4 × 22 cm/8½ inch dried rice paper rounds (available from Chinese food shops)

8 fresh coriander leaves

8 teaspoons chopped fresh chives

2 tablespoons groundnut oil

Lemon-, Coriander- and Tomato-flavoured oils, to serve (see opposite)

Cut the fish into 4 pieces about 7.5 cm/3 inches square. Combine the salt, five-pepper mixture and curry powder and sprinkle evenly over the fish pieces.

Mix the flour and water together to make a paste and set aside. Fill a large bowl with hot water and dip one of the rice paper rounds in it to soften; this will take only a few seconds. Remove and drain on a clean tea towel. In the centre of the round, place 2 coriander leaves, then a piece of fish and finally 2 teaspoons of chives. Fold the top edge over the ingredients, then fold in the sides. Fold the bottom edge over and seal with a little flour paste to secure the parcel. Repeat with the other 3 rounds to form 4 parcels.

Heat a large, heavy-based frying pan over a high heat until it is hot, then add the oil. When the oil is hot, add the 4 parcels and fry on the seamless side for about 3 minutes or until golden brown. Turn over and cook the other side until golden brown.

Now arrange the packages on a platter. Drizzle with a little of the flavoured oils and serve at once.

ingredients

3 tablespoons grated lemon zest

200 ml/7 fl oz groundnut or
vegetable oil

LEMON-FLAVOURED OIL

Put the lemon zest and oil in a blender or food processor
and mix for 1 minute. Transfer to a bowl, cover and
leave to stand for 2 days.

Strain the oil through a fine sieve. Use at once or store
tightly covered in the refrigerator for up to 6 months.
Bring to room temperature and shake before using.

ingredients

bunches of fresh coriander,
including stems, weighing about
100 g/4 oz

300 ml/½ pint extra virgin olive oil

CORIANDER-FLAVOURED OIL

Blanch the coriander in a large pan of boiling water for
15 seconds. Remove immediately and plunge into ice-
cold water. Drain well and pat dry with kitchen paper.
Put the blanched coriander and the olive oil in a blender
or food processor and process to a purée. Transfer to a
bowl, cover and leave to stand overnight.

Strain the mixture through a fine sieve. Use at once or
store tightly covered in the refrigerator for up to 2
weeks. Bring to room temperature and shake before
using.

ingredients

325 ml/11 fl oz extra virgin olive oil

3 tablespoons chopped garlic

1 tablespoon finely chopped
fresh ginger root

100 g/4 oz onions, chopped

100 g/4 oz celery, finely chopped

3 tablespoons coarsely chopped
fresh basil

1 tablespoon chopped fresh
oregano or 2 teaspoons
dried oregano

2 bay leaves

6 tablespoons tomato purée

8 tablespoons finely chopped
canned tomatoes

TOMATO-FLAVOURED OIL

Heat a non-stick wok or a large non-stick frying pan until
it is hot, then add 2 tablespoons of the olive oil. Add the
garlic, ginger, onions, celery and herbs and stir-fry for
5 minutes. Then add the tomato purée and chopped
tomatoes. Lower the heat and simmer for 15 minutes.
Now add the remaining olive oil and simmer for another
20 minutes. Remove from the heat and allow to cool
completely. Leave to stand overnight.

Strain through a fine sieve (the vegetable mixture can be
saved and used with pasta). Use at once or store tightly
covered in the refrigerator for up to 2 weeks. Bring to
room temperature before using.

Stir-fried chicken with chargrilled sweet peppers

This combines the Western technique of grilling or roasting peppers with the Chinese method of stir-frying.

ingredients

4 peppers, red, yellow and green

2 tablespoons extra virgin olive oil

450 g/1 lb boneless chicken breasts, skinned and cut into strips

1 egg white

1 teaspoon salt

3 teaspoons cornflour

300 ml/½ pint groundnut oil or water, plus 1 tablespoon groundnut oil

2 tablespoons finely sliced garlic

150 ml/¼ pint chicken stock, preferably home-made

2 teaspoons chilli bean sauce

2 teaspoons sugar

1½ tablespoons Shaoxing rice wine or dry sherry

1 tablespoon light soy sauce

shredded spring onions, to garnish

Using tongs, hold each pepper directly over the flame of a gas hob until the skin has blackened all over. If you don't have a gas hob, put them under a hot grill, turning occasionally. Place in a plastic bag and close it tightly. When the peppers have cooled, remove from the bag and peel off the charred skin. Clean the insides and discard the seeds. Cut the peppers into long strips, drizzle with the olive oil and set aside.

Mix the chicken with the egg white, salt and 2 teaspoons of the cornflour in a small bowl; refrigerate it for about 20 minutes.

If using oil, heat a wok or large frying pan over a high heat until hot, then add the oil. When it is very hot, remove the wok or pan from the heat and immediately add the chicken pieces, stirring vigorously to keep them from sticking. When they turn white, after about 2 minutes, quickly drain the chicken in a stainless steel colander set in a bowl. Discard the oil.

If you choose to use water instead of oil, bring it to the boil in a pan. Remove the pan from the heat and immediately add the chicken pieces, stirring vigorously to keep them from sticking. When the chicken pieces turn white, after about 2 minutes, quickly drain them in a colander set in a bowl. Discard the water.

Wipe the wok or pan clean and reheat until it is very hot. Then add the tablespoon of oil. When very hot, add the garlic and stir-fry for 2 minutes or until golden brown. Then add the stock, chilli bean sauce, sugar, rice wine or sherry and soy sauce. Cook for another 2 minutes. Mix the remaining cornflour with 1 tablespoon of water, add to the pan and cook for 20 seconds; add the chicken and pepper strips and stir-fry for another 2 minutes, coating the chicken thoroughly with the sauce. Garnish with shredded spring onions and serve at once.

Warmed berry compote with basil

Inspired by the English summer pudding, this works to perfection only when berries are at their peak of flavour. It is a refreshing and simple dessert to make and is delicious warm or cold. Any combination of berries in season will work well, and the more variety the better. If you use a wok, make sure it is a non-stick one so that the acid of the berries does not react with the carbon steel.

Bring the sugar and water to the boil in a non-stick or coated wok or pan, add the vanilla pod and simmer for 10 minutes. Remove the vanilla pod, rinse and save for future use.

Add the berries and butter to the sugar syrup and simmer for 2 minutes, just enough to warm but not to cook them. Remove from the heat, add the basil and stir gently. Transfer to a warm bowl and serve at once, with cream or vanilla ice cream.

ingredients

100 g/4 oz sugar

150 ml/¼ pint water

1 vanilla pod, split in half lengthways

75 g/3 oz strawberries

75 g/3 oz raspberries

75 g/3 oz blueberries

75 g/3 oz blackberries

25 g/1 oz unsalted butter

3 fresh basil leaves, finely shredded

cream or vanilla ice cream, to serve

Madhur Jaffrey taught herself to cook when, as a drama student at London's RADA, she could not find any Indian restaurants serving authentic food and asked her mother to send her recipes from home in Delhi. In 1982 she presented the BBC television series 'Indian Cookery', which did much to demystify Indian cooking for a British audience and went on to become hugely successful worldwide. Since then she has made two more series, 'Far Eastern Cookery' and 'Flavours of India', and written many bestselling books, including *A Taste of India, Madhur Jaffrey's Spice Kitchen* and *The Essential Madhur Jaffrey.*

Madhur Jaffrey also has a flourishing acting career, appearing in several Merchant-Ivory films and numerous radio and television plays.

Madhur Jaffrey

Madhur Jaffrey
cooks at
Edinburgh Castle

"I wanted the chefs to understand the concepts of blending herbs and spices – so essential to Indian cuisine."

menu

serves 4–6

Promila Kapoor's Paneer chat
  Spicy fresh cheese snack

Bhagari jhinga
  Prawns in a creamy aromatic sauce

Nishrin Attarwala's Kari
  Lamb in a cashew nut sauce
Khatte meethe baigan
  *Aubergine baked in a sweet and
  sour tamarind sauce*

Sev ka murabba
  *Caramelized cardamom apples
  with pistachio cream*

wine suggestions

Château de Rayne-Vigneau,
  AC 1er Cru Sauternes 1990

Mersault de Ropiteau AC 1993

Vino Nobile de Montepulciano,
  Poliziano 1993

Mercier Demi-Sec Champagne NV

Promila Kapoor's Paneer chat

Spicy fresh cheese snack

This absolutely delightful dish may be served as a snack, as an accompaniment for drinks or as a first course at a more formal meal. The cheese (*paneer*) is very like the Italian mozzarella.

Madhur Jaffrey

ingredients

FOR THE CHEESE:

1.75 litres/3 pints/7½ cups full-fat (whole) milk

about 4 tablespoons white vinegar, or more as needed

YOU ALSO NEED:

2.5 cm/1 inch piece of fresh ginger, peeled and cut into minute dice

4 tablespoons finely chopped onion

4 tablespoons finely chopped tomato

1-2 fresh hot green chillies, finely chopped

2 tablespoons finely chopped fresh green coriander or mint, or a mixture of the two

1 teaspoon salt

freshly ground black pepper

½–1 teaspoon *Chaat Masala* (see below)

2-3 tablespoons lemon juice

ingredients

4 teaspoons lightly roasted and ground cumin seeds

1½ tablespoons *amchoor*

2 teaspoons cayenne pepper

1 teaspoon finely ground black pepper

¾ teaspoon finely ground black salt

1 teaspoon salt

Makes about 5 tablespoons

Make the cheese (paneer): Bring the milk to the boil in a heavy saucepan. As soon as it begins to froth, add the vinegar, stir it in and turn off the heat. The curds should separate from the whey – if they don't do so completely, bring the milk to the boil again and add another tablespoon or so of vinegar. Stir and turn the heat off.

Line a strainer with a large, doubled-up piece of cheesecloth. Set the strainer over a large bowl. Pour the contents of the saucepan into the strainer. Let the whey drain away. Lift up the four corners of the cheesecloth. Using one of the corners, tie up the cheese in the cheesecloth into a bundle. Put this bundle on a board set in the sink. Put a plate on the bundle. Now put a weight – such as a medium-sized pan filled with water – on the plate. Remove after 3-4 minutes. Untie the bundle. The cheese is ready. It can be refrigerated.

Combine in a bowl the ginger, onion, tomato, chillies, coriander or mint, salt and black pepper, *chaat masala* and lemon juice. Toss. Taste for the balance of the seasonings.

Cut the cheese into 3 mm/⅛ inch thick slices. Arrange the slices in a single layer on a serving dish or on several individual plates. Put a generous dollop of the onion-tomato mixture on top of each piece and serve immediately.

CHAAT MASALA

There are many versions of this throughout North India. Here is a Punjabi version.

Mix all the ingredients thoroughly, breaking up any lumps. Store in a tightly lidded jar.

At Master Class, we combined the Paneer Chat with the Fresh red chutney with almonds to create a truly flavoursome starter.

ingredients

85 g/3 oz red pepper (about
half a de-seeded large one),
coarsely chopped

20 large mint leaves or 30 smaller
ones, coarsely chopped

2 tablespoons lemon juice

1 clove garlic, peeled and
coarsely chopped

½ teaspoon chilli powder

½ teaspoon salt

freshly ground black pepper

1 tablespoon blanched, chopped
or slivered almonds

1 teaspoon chopped dill (optional)

serves 8

LAL CHUTNEY

Fresh red chutney with almonds

I now like this chutney so much that I serve it with
most of my meals. Instead of fresh, hot red chillies,
I have used a combination of red pepper and chilli
powder. You may use the former, if you so wish. It
will be much hotter. Also, walnuts may be used
instead of the almonds. Both would be traditional
and authentic. This chutney may be kept in the
refrigerator for a few days.

Into the container of an electric blender, put the red
pepper, mint, lemon juice, garlic, chilli powder, salt and
black pepper in the order listed. Blend until smooth. Add
the almonds and blend again. A few bits of almond may
be left unpulverized. Pour into a bowl and check for
seasonings. You may now mix in the dill, if you wish.

Bhagari jhinga

Prawns in a creamy aromatic sauce

Mustard seeds are dropped into very hot oil for a few seconds to allow them to pop and turn nutty, some garlic is stirred in, and then peeled prawns are added and tossed with the garlic and mustard until they are almost done. With the addition of some salt, black pepper and cayenne, this could be a simple dish in itself. Instead comes the silken sauce – a tomato and cream base with the earthy addition of ground roasted cumin, pungent fresh ginger, lemon juice and the aromatic garam masala.The sauce can be made ahead of time and refrigerated. The prawns can be peeled, deveined, washed, patted dry and left covered in the refrigerator. The actual cooking takes just a few minutes. This dish is best served with rice.

ingredients

FOR THE SAUCE:

250 ml/8 fl oz tomato sauce or passata

¾ teaspoon salt

1 teaspoon ground garam masala

½ teaspoon ground roasted cumin seeds

pinch cayenne pepper, or to taste

1 teaspoon fresh ginger, peeled and very finely grated

3 tablespoons green coriander, finely chopped

1 fresh, long hot green chilli, finely chopped

1 tablespoon lemon juice

250 ml/8 fl oz double cream

FOR THE PRAWNS:

3 tablespoons vegetable oil

1 teaspoon brown mustard seeds

3 garlic cloves, peeled and finely chopped

550 g/1¼ lb medium prawns, peeled and deveined, washed and patted dry

Put the tomato sauce in a bowl. Add the salt, *garam masala*, ground cumin, cayenne, ginger, coriander, chilli, lemon juice and cream. Mix well, cover, and set aside, refrigerating if necessary.

Just before you sit down to eat, heat the oil in a wok or a frying pan over fairly high heat. When hot, add the mustard seeds. As soon as the mustard seeds begin to pop – this takes just a few seconds – add the garlic. Stir briefly, until the garlic turns medium-brown, then add the prawns. Stir until the prawns turn opaque most of the way through, then add the sauce. Turn the heat to medium and heat the sauce through just until it begins to simmer. By then the prawns should be completely opaque and cooked through. Turn off the heat. Serve.

Nishrin Attarwala's Kari

Lamb in a cashew nut sauce

The Bohris of Gujarat, a Muslim community, cook some of the best meat dishes on the west coast of India. This is one of their specialities. It is served with Black Pepper Rice, which helps to absorb the absolutely wonderful sauce. It is really the sauce that makes the dish. Rich with a ground mixture of nuts – cashews, the hazelnut-like charoli nut (sold by Indian grocers) and roasted peanuts – seeds such as watermelon seeds and spices such as star anise and cloves, it is both uncommon and good. If you cannot get any of the more unusual nuts or seeds, just increase the cashews or peanuts by a similar amount. This dish may also be made with chicken, which should be skinned and cut into 5 cm/2 inch pieces. Each of the two cooking stages would be 12-15 minutes.

Madhur Jaffrey

ingredients

FOR THE NUT, SEED AND SPICE MIXTURE:

2 tablespoons raw cashew nuts,
split or broken

2 tablespoons *charoli* (*chironji*)

1½ tablespoons roasted peanuts

1½ tablespoons roasted chick peas,
or roasted *chana dal*

1½ tablespoons peeled watermelon seeds

1 teaspoon cumin seeds

7-8 cloves

1 teaspoon black peppercorns

1 teaspoon ground coriander

2.5 cm/1 inch cinnamon stick, broken

6-7 dried hot red chillies

2 star anise

¼ teaspoon ground turmeric

FOR THE FIRST COOKING STAGE:

4 tablespoons vegetable oil

2 medium-large red onions (225 g/
8 oz), finely sliced

2.5 cm/1 inch piece of fresh ginger,
finely chopped

5-6 garlic cloves, peeled and
finely chopped

4 fresh hot green chillies, finely chopped

450 g/1 lb boned lamb from the shoulder,
cut into 4 cm/1½ inch cubes)

½ teaspoon salt

FOR THE SECOND COOKING STAGE:

3 tablespoons vegetable oil

1 teaspoon cumin seeds

20-30 fresh curry leaves, if available

2.5 cm/1 inch cinnamon stick

2-3 cloves

½ teaspoon black peppercorns

2-3 garlic cloves, peeled and chopped

2 large ripe tomatoes, puréed in an
electric blender

400 ml/14 fl oz/1¾ cups coconut milk,
from a well-stirred can, thinned with
300 ml/10 fl oz/1¼ cups water

½ teaspoon salt

3 tablespoons lemon juice

3 tablespoons finely chopped,
fresh green coriander

Put the ingredients for the nut, seed and spice mixture into a clean coffee grinder. Grind to a fine powder. Empty into a bowl. Add 5-6 tablespoons water to make a thick paste. Set aside.

For the first cooking stage: Heat the 4 tablespoons oil in a large, wide, preferably non-stick pan or wok over medium-high heat. When hot, add the onions. Stir and fry for 3-4 minutes or until they turn brown at the edges. Add the ginger, garlic and chillies. Stir and fry for a minute. Put in the lamb and ½ teaspoon salt. Stir and fry for 2-3 minutes. Add the spice paste and 450 ml/ 15 fl oz/2 cups water. Bring to the boil. Cover, turn the heat to low and cook for 55 minutes.

For the second cooking stage: Heat the 3 tablespoons oil in a clean wide pan or wok over medium-high heat. When hot, add the cumin seeds, curry leaves, cinnamon, cloves and peppercorns. Stir for 10 seconds. Add the garlic. Stir and fry until the garlic starts to brown. Now add the lamb and the sauce from the first pan, along with the tomato purée, stirred coconut milk, salt and lemon juice. Stir to mix.

Cook over medium-high heat for about 10-15 minutes until the lamb is tender and the sauce has become thick.

Sprinkle with the fresh coriander to garnish.

*left: Khatte meethe baigan (top), page 96;
Nishrin Attarwala's Kari (bottom)*

Madhur Jaffrey

Khatte meethe baigan

Aubergine baked in a sweet-and-sour tamarind sauce

Madhur Jaffrey

In this recipe, aubergine are grilled, brushed with a sweet-and-sour tamarind chutney, and baked; it is as simple as that. The tamarind chutney is the key here. The naturally tangy taste of tamarind combined with the nutty, musky aroma of roasted and ground cumin seeds is quite irresistible. I use the slim, long, pinkish-mauve aubergines that are sometimes called Japanese aubergines. If you cannot find them, use the large oval ones. Just cut them crossways into rounds. Bake the aubergines in the dish in which you will serve them. I use an oval dish that is about 25 cm/10 inches long and about 6 cm/2½ inches high, but you could just as easily use a square or rectangular dish. Rice should be served on the side.

ingredients

1.25 kg/2½ lb aubergine

6-8 tablespoons vegetable oil

salt

freshly ground black pepper

3 tablespoons tamarind chutney (see below), diluted with 3 tablespoons water

At Master Class, the chutney was made without the bananas to form part of the Aubergine dish above.

Pre-heat the grill. Cut the aubergine somewhat diagonally into 8 mm/⅜ inch-thick slices. Brush generously on both sides with oil. Sprinkle each side lightly with salt and pepper as well. Put as many slices as will fit in a single layer on the grill rack and cook on both sides until golden brown. Repeat for remaining aubergine.

Pre-heat the oven to 180°C/350°F/Gas Mark 4. Arrange the aubergine slices in a baking dish in slightly overlapping rows. When the bottom is covered with a layer of slices, drizzle a third of the chutney over them and spread it evenly with your fingers. Cover the first layer with two more layers of aubergine, coating each with the chutney. Cover the baking dish with foil and bake for 20 minutes.

TAMARIND CHUTNEY

This is another sweet and sour chutney made with tamarind pulp. The addition of roasted cumin and slices of ripe bananas is, I think, very particular to Delhi dwellers. My mother's family often added raisins as well. I have not included them in my recipe, but if you wish to do so, soak a tablespoon of golden raisins in hot water for 2 hours. Then remove them from the water and add them to the tamarind pulp at the same time that you add the bananas.

ingredients

a piece of tamarind, the size
of a tangerine

1-1½ tablespoons sugar

1¼ teaspoons salt

1 teaspoon roasted, ground
cumin seeds

⅛–¼ teaspoon cayenne pepper
(optional)

1 ripe but firm banana, peeled and
sliced into ¼–⅓ inch slices

To serve: Put into a small
ceramic or glass serving bowl
and place on the table along
with other chutneys and pickles

Since the tamarind generally comes in a large block, tear off a lump about the size of a tangerine. Soak it overnight in 175 ml/6 fl oz hot water in a small non-metallic bowl or cup. (The water should cover the tamarind, so don't use a very wide bowl.) If you forget to do it overnight, do it first thing in the morning. All will not be lost! Soak it for a minimum of 4 hours. Once it has soaked, mash down and break the lump in the water, making a thick, uneven pulp. I use my hands for this, but you could use the back of a wooden spoon.

Place a strainer over a non-metallic bowl, put the tamarind pulp in the strainer, and press down with the back of a spoon. Keep pressing until nothing but fibrous tissues and seeds are left in the strainer. Discard fibrous tissues and seeds. Make sure you scrape all the strained pulp on the outside of the strainer – it doesn't always drip down. Use extra water, if necessary, to separate all the pulp from the fibres. Mix the strained pulp with the sugar, salt, cumin seeds, cayenne and bananas.

Madhur Jaffrey

Sev ka murabba

Caramelised cardamom apples with pistachio cream

An easy dessert that can be made with any sour, firm apples such as Granny Smiths. It may be served hot or warm.

ingredients

FOR THE CREAM:

250 ml/8 fl oz double cream for
whipping

2 tablespoons pistachios, finely
chopped

FOR THE APPLES:

115 g/4 oz unsalted butter

4 medium-sized sour, firm apples

¼ teaspoon finely ground
cardamom seeds

⅛ teaspoon ground cinnamon

⅛ teaspoon ground cloves

140 g/5 oz sugar

3 tablespoon blanched, slivered
almonds

2 tablespoons chopped walnuts

Whip the cream lightly until it just holds shape but is not stiff at all. Fold half of the pistachio nuts into the cream. Refrigerate the cream.

Melt the butter over low heat in a large, non-stick frying pan. Take the pan off the heat. Peel, core and slice the apples thinly, dropping the slices into the butter as you cut them. Fold them into the butter as you go so that they do not discolour. (You could, if you like, keep the frying pan over very low heat as you do this.) Add the cardamom, cinnamon, cloves, sugar, almonds and walnuts. Cook on medium heat for 2-3 minutes, stirring gently as you do so. Now turn the heat to high. Cook for 8-10 minutes, stirring very gently now and then, until the apples have caramelized lightly.

Serve on individual plates with a dollop of the cream partially on and partially off the apples. Sprinkle the remaining chopped pistachios over the cream.

Alastair Little is a self-taught chef who worked at the London restaurants L'Escargot and 192 Kensington Park Road before opening his much-acclaimed eponymous restaurant in Frith Street, Soho, in 1982. This was followed in 1995 by a second restaurant, Alastair Little Lancaster Road.

He spends part of each summer running courses at La Cacciata, his cookery school in Umbria, upon which his book *Alastair Little's Italian Kitchen* is based. His other books include *Food of the Sun* and *Keep it Simple*, which won the Glenfiddich Food and Drink Book of the Year Award in 1994.

Alastair Little

Alastair Little
cooks on the Thames, aboard Symphony 2

"I am a great believer in the best ingredients, simply prepared."

menu

serves 4

Scallop and tiger prawn noodle
   salad

Wrapped breast of chicken with
   wild mushrooms and truffles

Fig and frangipane tart

wine suggestions

Sancerre, Château de Sancerre 1992

Calera Pinot Noir 1992

Château Climens Premier Cru
   Classe, Barsac

Scallop and tiger prawn noodle salad

Ask your fishmonger to open the scallop shells and detach the meat for you. Never buy frozen or pre-shelled scallops; they just aren't worth cooking, never mind eating.

Alastair Little

ingredients

12 medium-sized scallops

12 raw tiger prawns

225 g/8 oz rice noodles

4 tablespoons rice wine vinegar or white wine vinegar

2 lemongrass stalks, cut into very fine strips

2 kaffir lime leaves

2 large red chillies, finely sliced

125 ml/4 fl oz sunflower oil, plus more for brushing

1 onion, cut into thin rings

1 garlic clove, cut into fine strips

1 red pepper, roasted, peeled and finely shredded

2.5 cm/1 inch piece of fresh ginger root, cut into fine strips

1 carrot, cut into fine strips

1 small Savoy cabbage, finely shredded

4 tablespoons Kikkoman soy sauce

1 tablespoon Thai fish sauce (*nam pla*)

a bunch of fresh coriander

1 tablespoon sesame oil

Prepare the scallops and prawns: detach the corals from the scallops – these can be used in a fish soup. Cut the white flesh in half horizontally. Shell the prawns, leaving the tail shell on, and remove the intestinal vein running along the back.

Put the rice noodles in a bowl, pour over boiling water and leave to soak according to the manufacturer's instructions. Drain well.

Heat the vinegar in a saucepan and simmer the lemongrass, kaffir lime leaves and red chillies in it for 5 minutes, then set aside.

Heat a wok and when hot put in half the sunflower oil. Add the onion, garlic, red pepper, ginger and carrot. Toss and stir. Add the cabbage and toss again. Add the noodles and toss, then quickly pour in the vinegar mixture, the rest of the oil, the soy and fish sauce. Boil, toss and stir. Tip into a bowl and leave to cool.

When ready to serve, chop the coriander and stir it into the salad.

Put a griddle pan to heat. Brush the prawns lightly with a little sunflower oil and grill for about 3 minutes, until pink. Remove from the pan. Brush the scallop halves with oil and sear them for no more than 30 seconds on each side. Longer will toughen them.

To serve, mound the salad on 4 plates and arrange the scallops and prawns on top. Dress each with a few drops of the sesame oil.

Authors' Note: This recipe is adapted from the original recipe which appeared in *Keep It Simple* © 1993 by Alastair Little and Richard Whittington, reprinted by permission of Conran Octopus Ltd..

Wrapped breast of chicken with wild mushrooms and truffles

Alastair Little

ingredients

50 g/2 oz dried morels

25 g/1 oz dried ceps

8 large leaves of seasonal green or Savoy cabbage (outer leaves only)

225 g/8 oz butter

8 slices of pancetta or 4 of prosciutto (ask the grocer to cut on number-two thickness)

4 large chicken supremes (skinless breasts with wingbone attached)

300 ml/½ pint chicken stock

1 glass (150 ml/¼ pint) dry white wine

2 shallots, finely chopped

salt and freshly ground black pepper

a few shavings of fresh truffle, to serve (optional)

Put the dried mushrooms to soak in warm water for half an hour. Blanch the cabbage leaves in a large pan of boiling salted water for 3 minutes, then refresh in cold water. Drain thoroughly and cut out the tough bottom part of the stalk from each leaf. Butter four 20 cm/8 inch squares of foil. Spread 2 of the green leaves on each foil square to cover. Place 2 slices of pancetta slightly overlapping or 1 slice of prosciutto on top to cover as much of the greens as possible. Then place a 15 g/ ½ oz piece of butter in the middle and put a chicken supreme on it. Grind black pepper to season, but add no salt as the ham is salty and the taste will be intensified when hot. Carefully fold the greens and ham around the supreme, then roll the foil around.

Drain the reconstituted mushrooms into a saucepan through a fine sieve or butter muslin. Chop the mushrooms and set aside. Add the chicken stock and white wine to the soaking liquid and boil to reduce to 600 ml/1 pint.

Generously butter a roasting tin just large enough to hold the chicken packages. Distribute the chopped shallots evenly over the base of the tin. Scatter the reconstituted mushrooms over the shallots. Arrange the 4 packages on top and pour the hot stock over them. Bake for 30 minutes in an oven preheated to its highest setting. Remove from the oven and transfer the packages to a hot dish. Leave to rest in a warm place for 10 minutes while you make the sauce.

Strain the stock and set the mushrooms aside in a warm place. Return the stock to the roasting tin. Cut the remaining butter into small pieces. Put the roasting tin on the hob, bring the contents to a rolling boil and boil until reduced to about 150 ml/¼ pint. Adjust the seasoning, then whisk in the butter a piece at a time until amalgamated. Remove from the heat and stir in the mushrooms.

To serve, unwrap the foil from the chicken and carve each supreme into 3 pieces. Pour the sauce on 4 heated plates and arrange the pieces, overlapping, in the centre of each. Garnish with shavings of fresh truffle, if using, and serve immediately.

Authors' Note: This recipe is adapted from the original recipe which appeared in *Keep it Simple* © 1993 by Alastair Little and Richard Whittington, reprinted by permission of Conran Octopus Ltd.

Fig and frangipane tart

The exact number of figs you need will depend on their size. They should be ripe but still firm. Tinned figs also taste good cooked this way but remember to drain them carefully before halving and pushing into the frangipane. The lengthy blind-baking is needed if the pastry is to be a deep nut-brown when the tart finally emerges from the oven. At the risk of offending Mr Kipling, an anaemic appearance is to be avoided at all costs.

Alastair Little

ingredients

about 450 g/1 lb ripe figs
(or drained tinned)

2–3 tablespoons Hymettus or other fine, clear, non-floral honey, to glaze

Greek yoghurt, whipped cream or crème fraîche, to serve

FOR THE LEMON AND ALMOND PASTRY SHELL:

125 g/4½ oz caster sugar

50 g/2 oz ground almonds

125 g/4½ oz fine plain flour

100 g/4 oz butter, cut into small cubes

1 medium egg, plus 1 extra yolk

2 teaspoons finely grated lemon zest

1 teaspoon Pernod or Pastis

a pinch of salt

FOR THE FRANGIPANE:

50 g/2 oz butter

50 g/2 oz caster sugar

50 g/2 oz ground almonds

50 g/2 oz fresh white breadcrumbs

1 large egg

3 drops of almond essence

For the pastry shell, put the sugar, almonds and flour into a food processor and turn it on at full speed for a few seconds. Add the diced butter and work again until just blended in. The mixture will resemble fine breadcrumbs. Add the egg and extra yolk, the lemon zest, Pernod or Pastis and a tiny pinch of salt and work again until the pastry balls. Scrape this out on to a sheet of clingfilm and form into a cylinder about 5 cm/2 inches in diameter. Chill for at least 2 hours.

The pastry is very rich and you will need to flour the work surface heavily to prevent it sticking; it is not easy to roll. If it defeats you, cut thin discs off the end of the cylinder and press these into the bottom and sides of a 24 cm/9½ inch loose-bottomed metal tart tin to make as even a pastry shell as possible. Give a double thickness round the edges and push it right up to the top, as it will shrink as it bakes. Be careful to press into the bottom edges to eliminate air between the tin and the pastry. Freeze until needed.

For the frangipane, put the butter, sugar, almonds and breadcrumbs in a food processor and work briefly to mix. On full speed, add the egg and almond essence until combined to a smooth paste.

Take the pastry shell from the freezer and put it on a baking tray. Prick the base all over with a fork and line the shell with foil. Fill with beans and bake blind in an oven preheated to 190°C/375°F/Gas Mark 5 for 25–30 minutes, removing the foil and beans for the last 10 minutes. Remove the cooked shell from the oven and leave to cool slightly before filling with the almond paste. Scrape the surface smooth and level.

Authors' Note: This recipe is adapted from the original recipe which appeared in *Food of the Sun* © 1995 by Alastair Little and Richard Whittington, published by Quadrille Publishing Ltd.

Cut the figs in half, make shallow slashes in the skins with a razor blade (if using tinned figs, do not slash) and press into the paste, cut-side up, in concentric circles slightly overlapping.

Bake for 45–60 minutes, when the figs will have crumpled a little and the frangipane will have risen around them. The cooking time is slowed by the liquid exuding from the figs and the amount of liquid will depend on how ripe they are. It is therefore impossible to be precise about cooking times. Check periodically by pressing the centre with a finger to gauge whether the frangipane is set firm. Cover the edges of the flan loosely with foil if the pastry gets too brown.

Remove the tart from the oven when done. Put the honey into a pan and heat gently to liquefy. Brush the figs with it. Serve the tart warm, with spoonfuls of Greek yoghurt, whipped cream or crème fraîche.

Paul Rankin was born in County Down, Northern Ireland, Jeanne in Winnipeg, Canada. They worked in restaurants around the world before receiving a classical culinary training under Albert Roux in London. After spells in Canada and California they finally settled in Belfast, opening their restaurant, Roscoff, in 1989. Combining Californian style with lovingly chosen Irish produce, Roscoff became the first restaurant in Northern Ireland to win a Michelin star.

The Rankins' television series 'Gourmet Ireland' and 'Gourmet Ireland Two' were accompanied by bestselling books. They have also produced the innovative *Hot Food Cool Jazz* – a recipe book packaged with a jazz CD featuring Jeanne's jazz musician brother, Marc LeBrun.

Paul and Jeanne Rankin

Paul and Jeanne Rankin
cook at Kenley House

"The chefs are keen to learn, so we try to include techniques that they will find useful; but it's equally important that the day is enjoyable as well as informative."

menu 1

serves 6

Blackened monkfish with
  curried aubergine

Crispy duck confit with balsamic
  lentils and roast pimentos

Peach and raspberry tiramisù

wine suggestions

Bouché Père et Fils, Cuvée Réservée, Brut

Argyle Dry Reserve Riesling 1990/2

Pomino Rosso, Pomino,
  Frescobaldi 1990/1

Heggies Vineyard Eden Valley
  Botrytis Riesling 1991

Blackened monkfish
with curried aubergine

Blackened fish is one of the most famous dishes of New Orleans. Here the technique has been adapted for the home cook. It is no less delicious, however, even if it is a little bit smoky.

ingredients

700 g/1½ lb monkfish fillet, cut into 6

2 tablespoons light olive oil

FOR THE BLACKENING SEASONINGS:

1 teaspoon salt

½ teaspoon dried oregano

½ teaspoon dried thyme

½ teaspoon black pepper

¼ teaspoon white pepper

¼ teaspoon onion powder

¼ teaspoon garlic powder

¼ teaspoon cayenne pepper

¼ teaspoon paprika

FOR THE CURRIED AUBERGINE:

4 tablespoons light olive oil

1 large aubergine, cut into 1 cm/½ inch dice

1 large onion, thinly sliced

1 green chilli, deseeded and chopped

1 teaspoon hot curry powder

2 tablespoons chopped fresh coriander

salt and freshly ground black pepper

First prepare the aubergine. Heat 3 tablespoons of the oil in a large frying pan over a high heat, add the aubergine and sauté for about 6 minutes or until nicely browned and quite soft. Drain on kitchen paper.

Heat the remaining oil in a separate pan, add the onion and chilli and cook gently for about 5 minutes, until soft. Stir in the curry powder and cook for 2 minutes. Now stir in the aubergine and cook for a further 2 minutes. Mix in the coriander, season to taste and keep warm.

Combine all the blackening seasonings in a small bowl. Drizzle the monkfish fillets with 1 tablespoon of the oil and then rub the seasoning spices into them.

Heat a large, heavy-based frying pan over a high heat until almost smoking. Add the remaining oil, then the monkfish fillets. Cook for about 3 minutes on each side. This is a slightly smoky process but continue cooking until the seasonings 'blacken'. Serve immediately, on a bed of the curried aubergine.

Crispy duck confit with balsamic lentils and roast pimentos

ingredients

6 duck legs

2 litres/2½ pints duck or goose fat

1 large red pepper

1 large yellow pepper

1 tablespoon light olive oil

salt and freshly ground
black pepper

FOR THE MARINADE:

6 large garlic cloves, crushed

2 tablespoons coarse sea salt

1 tablespoon cracked
black peppercorns

2 bay leaves, crumbled

2 fresh thyme sprigs,
roughly chopped

1 fresh rosemary sprig,
roughly chopped

FOR THE BALSAMIC LENTILS:

225 g/8 oz green or brown lentils

600 ml/1 pint water

2 tablespoons finely chopped onion

1 tablespoon finely diced carrot

1 tablespoon finely diced leek

1 bay leaf

a pinch of dried thyme

600 ml/1 pint brown chicken stock

150 ml/¼ pint balsamic vinegar

150 ml/¼ pint virgin olive oil

1 teaspoon chopped fresh rosemary

1 tablespoon chopped fresh parsley

1 teaspoon cracked black
peppercorns

1 teaspoon salt

Scatter the marinade ingredients evenly over the duck legs, then cover and marinate in the fridge for up to 24 hours. Turn the legs periodically over this period to ensure an even flavour.

To cook the duck, rinse off the marinade ingredients and pat the legs dry. Melt the duck or goose fat in a heavy casserole, immerse the duck legs in it and cook gently for 1½ hours or until very tender.

Meanwhile, prepare the lentils. Wash the lentils and put them in a pot with the water. Bring to the boil and simmer for 5 minutes, skimming off the scum that rises to the surface. Add the chopped vegetables, bay leaf and thyme and simmer until the lentils are just tender. Simmer the brown chicken stock in a separate pan until reduced by half its volume. When the lentils are done, make sure they are not too watery, pouring off any excess liquid if necessary, then stir in the chicken stock, balsamic vinegar, olive oil, herbs, black pepper and salt. Keep the lentils warm.

Rub the red and yellow peppers with the olive oil and grill (or roast) them over a high heat until blistered and blackened on all sides. Remove from the heat and leave until cool enough to handle, then peel off the skin. Halve and deseed the peppers, and cut into strips. Season with salt and pepper.

Crisp the confit legs under a hot grill, skin-side up, or in a heavy frying pan, skin-side down, or for 5 minutes in an oven preheated to 200°C/400°F/Gas Mark 6. Generously ladle the lentils into the middle of warm serving plates or bowls. Scatter a few peppers over them and top with the confit legs.

This can be served with a few grilled potatoes and a salad of rocket.

Peach and raspberry tiramisù

ingredients

6 fresh peaches, poached
(or use canned peaches)

6 tablespoons peach brandy

2 punnets of raspberries
(175–225 g/6–8 oz each punnet)

285 g/10 oz sugar

2–3 tablespoons lemon juice

450 g/1 lb mascarpone cheese

3 eggs, separated

1 gelatine leaf, softened in
cold water

175 g/6 oz Savoiardi biscuits
or sponge fingers

mint sprigs and candied lemon
zest (optional), to decorate

FOR THE PASTRY CREAM:

250 ml/8 fl oz milk

½ vanilla pod

65 g/2½ oz caster sugar

3 egg yolks

20 g/¾ oz plain flour, sifted

10 g/⅓ oz cornflour, sifted

icing sugar for dusting (optional)

First make the pastry cream: place the milk and vanilla pod in a pan and bring to the boil. Set aside to infuse. Whisk together the sugar and egg yolks until light and pale yellow. Whisk in the flour and cornflour and continue to whisk until smooth. Slowly pour some of the hot milk on to the egg mixture, whisking continuously. Whisk in the rest of the milk. Return it all to the pan and cook over a medium heat, whisking all the time, for 2–3 minutes, until it comes to the boil. Continue to whisk for another 2 minutes; this ensures that the flour is cooked through. Remove from the heat and strain through a fine sieve into a bowl. To help prevent a skin forming, either cover with a layer of clingfilm right on top of the pastry cream or heavily dust the top with icing sugar. When cool, the pastry cream can be stored in the fridge for 5 days. You will only need 150 g/5 oz for this recipe; the remainder can be used to fill all kinds of pastry desserts, from éclairs to puff pastries and fruit tarts.

Drain the poached or canned peaches, reserving the syrup. Halve, stone and slice the peaches and set aside on a piece of kitchen paper to absorb excess moisture. Add half the peach brandy to the syrup and reserve.

Set aside 6 nice raspberries for garnish and lightly mash the rest with 100 g/4 oz of the sugar and the lemon juice. What you want is a nice lumpy mash. Set aside.

Beat half of the mascarpone with a wooden spoon until soft. Stir in 150 g/5 oz of the pastry cream, 75 g/3 oz of the sugar and the remaining peach brandy. Set aside.

Place the egg yolks and 50 g/2 oz of the sugar in a mixing bowl set over a pan of simmering water and whisk until the mixture is pale yellow, feels slightly warmer than body temperature and trails off the whisk in ribbons. Drain the gelatine and whisk it into the yolk/sugar mixture. Remove the bowl from the heat and continue to whisk until the mixture is light and fluffy and no longer hot. This last step can be done in a mixer, with the whisk attachment, at about medium speed.

Beat the remaining mascarpone with a wooden spoon until soft, then fold it into the yolk/sugar mixture. Whisk the egg whites with the remaining sugar until thick and glossy and gently fold them into the yolk and mascarpone mixture.

To assemble, place 2 Savoiardi biscuits or sponge fingers in the bottom of each of 6 tall glass dishes, breaking them up to fit. Soak these heavily with the peach syrup. Next place a spoonful of the pastry cream/mascarpone on top, making sure there is enough to form a nice layer (but too much can be too heavy to eat). Carefully fan a layer of sliced peaches on top. Depending on the shape and size of the mould, this layer may be one or two thicknesses of peach slices. Top the peaches with the mashed raspberry purée. Finally, spoon on a good dollop of the light and fluffy mascarpone/egg mixture. Chill for at least an hour to let the flavours blend and to allow the mixtures to set a little. To serve, decorate with mint sprigs, the reserved raspberries and perhaps some candied lemon zest.

Paul and Jeanne Rankin
cook at Croke Park

"It is important that the food is produced to the same exacting standards as at Roscoff."

menu 2

serves 6

Sugar-cured cod on warm potato
  pancake with beetroot vinaigrette

Peppered leg of venison with hot
  and sour cabbage

Apple galettes with crème Chantilly

wine suggestions

Glen Ellen Proprietor's Reserve
  Chardonnay 1995

Rosemount Estate Show Reserve
  Cabernet Sauvignon 1995 Hunter Valley

Muscat de Beaume de Venise 1995 –
  M Chapoutier

Sugar-cured cod on warm potato pancake with beetroot vinaigrette

ingredients

500 g/1 lb 2 oz cod fillet, skinned

25 g/1 oz sugar

25 g/1 oz sel gris (grey sea salt)

5 white peppercorns, lightly crushed

2–3 tablespoons chopped fresh dill

fresh chervil and dill sprigs and long chive strands, to garnish

FOR THE BEETROOT VINAIGRETTE:

½ teaspoon salt

½ teaspoon freshly ground black pepper

2 teaspoons Dijon mustard

4 tablespoons white wine vinegar

225 ml/7½ fl oz vegetable or light olive oil

2 small cooked beetroot (about 65 g/2½ oz), cut into 1 cm/½ inch dice

FOR THE CHIVE CRÈME FRAÎCHE:

250 g/9 oz crème fraîche

1 bunch of fresh chives, finely chopped

lemon juice

FOR THE POTATO PANCAKES:

250 g/9 oz floury potatoes, peeled and chopped

2 tablespoons plain flour

2 eggs, separated

about 4 tablespoons double cream

25 g/1 oz butter

salt and freshly ground white pepper

Prepare the cod in advance. Sprinkle the sugar, salt and pepper evenly over the fillets. Sprinkle the dill on top, wrap in clingfilm, then marinate in the fridge for 24–36 hours. Every few hours turn the fish over and drain off any liquid. Remove all the marinade ingredients and pat the fillet dry. Cut into 6 equal pieces.

To make the vinaigrette, dissolve the salt, pepper and mustard in the vinegar. Gradually whisk in the oil. Place some of the vinaigrette in a blender with half the beetroot and whizz to a purée. Mix with the rest of the vinaigrette, then toss in the rest of the beetroot. (Or you can purée all the beetroot for a thicker vinaigrette.)

Mix the crème fraîche with the chives and a few drops of lemon juice, adding some salt and pepper to taste.

To make the pancakes, cook the potatoes until tender, drain well and mash until smooth. Gently stir in the flour, then the egg yolks. Beat in just enough cream, one spoon at a time, to give a thick batter consistency, like a medium porridge. Do not add all the cream if the batter is thin enough (this will depend on the amount of water absorbed by the potatoes during cooking). Whisk the egg whites to very soft peaks and fold them into the batter.

To cook, heat a small cast-iron frying pan over gentle heat until very hot. Add some of the butter, let it foam, then add a large spoonful of the batter. It will spread and find its own thickness. Cook for 3–4 minutes, until beginning to set. Turn it over and cook for 2 minutes. Place in a warm oven, still in the frying pan, for a minute or two. This is not absolutely necessary but ensures that the pancake is cooked through. Drain on kitchen paper and cook the rest in the remaining butter in the same way.

To cook the cod, sear the fillets quickly in hot pans. Place a piece of cod on top of a pancake in the centre of each serving plate. Sprinkle the vinaigrette around the pancakes, place a quenelle of the chive crème fraîche on top of the cod and garnish it all with a few sprigs of chervil and dill and some long strands of chive.

Peppered leg of venison with hot and sour cabbage

In this recipe you need to separate the leg muscles out of the haunch of venison, which means that you are left with sinew-free 'loin' from the leg. If you prefer you could use 6 venison fillet steaks.

ingredients

1 haunch of venison, weighing about 2.5 kg/5½ lb

cracked black peppercorns

25 g/1 oz butter

1 tablespoon vegetable oil

60 ml/2 fl oz sherry vinegar

60 ml/2 fl oz meat stock or gravy (optional)

300 ml/½ pint double cream

salt and freshly ground black pepper

FOR THE HOT AND SOUR CABBAGE:

25 g/1oz butter

1 red cabbage, finely sliced

60 ml/2 fl oz sherry vinegar

salt

2 eating apples, peeled, cored and chopped

2 tablespoons raisins

1 tablespoon chopped fresh ginger root

½ teaspoon freshly ground white pepper

sugar to taste

First prepare the cabbage: melt the butter in a large, heavy casserole, add the cabbage, vinegar and some salt, then cover and cook over a low heat for about 1 hour. Stir in the apples, raisins, ginger and some sugar and cook slowly for another 30 minutes. Finally add the white pepper and check the seasoning to see if it needs more sugar or salt. Keep warm.

Trim the outside of the venison haunch to remove any sinew and fat, working carefully so that you don't remove too much flesh. Separate each large muscle, one at a time, and place to one side. (Reserve the trimmings, shin and very small muscles for another use.) Roll the large muscles in some cracked black pepper and season them with salt.

Heat a large ovenproof frying pan and sauté the pieces of venison in the butter and oil until they have a nice colour on all sides. Transfer to an oven preheated to 190°C/375°F/Gas Mark 5 and cook for about 5 minutes for medium rare or 8 minutes for medium well done. Remove the venison pieces from the pan and leave to rest in a warm place. Pour any fat from the pan, add the sherry vinegar and scrape the bottom of the pan with a wooden spoon to loosen all the delicious, caramelized juices. Boil until the vinegar is reduced to about 1 tablespoon, then add the stock or gravy, if using, and the cream. Boil until it has reduced and thickened to a sauce consistency. Season with salt and pepper.

To serve, slice the venison pieces. Spoon some piping hot cabbage on to warmed plates and arrange the slices neatly on top. Pour over a little of the sauce and it's ready to go.

Apple galettes with crème Chantilly

ingredients

450 g/1 lb puff pastry

3 apples

3 tablespoons lemon juice

2 egg yolks, mixed with
4 teaspoons water

6–9 tablespoons sugar

1½ teaspoons finely grated
lemon zest

¾ teaspoon ground cinnamon

50–75 g/2–3 oz butter,
cut into small dice

175 g/6 oz apricot jam, melted with
a little water and then sieved

FOR THE CRÈME CHANTILLY:

250 ml/8 fl oz double cream

½ teaspoon vanilla extract

1–2 tablespoons icing sugar

Roll out the pastry to about 5 mm/¼ inch thick. Cut out 6 rounds. Place them on an ungreased baking sheet and chill for at least 30 minutes.

Meanwhile, make the crème Chantilly: whip the cream until it starts to thicken, add the vanilla and icing sugar to taste and continue to whip until the cream thickens lightly again. Chill until needed.

Peel and core the apples, then slice them very thinly, tossing them in the lemon juice as you go to avoid discoloration. Set aside.

Remove the pastry from the fridge and prick it all over with a fork. Bake in an oven preheated to 200°C/400°F/ Gas Mark 6 for about 10 minutes, until golden and crisp. Leave to cool.

Brush the cooled pastry lightly with the egg yolk mixed with water (to seal) and arrange the apple slices on top in an attractive overlapping fashion, covering the whole surface. Mix the sugar with the lemon zest and cinnamon. Generously sprinkle the sugar over the apple and place dots of butter randomly on top. Put the galettes back in the oven for about 15–20 minutes, until the apples are cooked through and lightly coloured. Remove from the oven.

Warm the apricot jam again if necessary, until runny. While the galettes are still warm, lightly brush the jam over the apple slices. This gives a lovely shine to the fruit and a professional finish to the galettes. Serve warm, with a scoop of crème Chantilly.

Gary Rhodes' early career included time at the Amsterdam Hilton, the Capital Hotel in Knightsbridge, the Castle Hotel, Somerset and the Greenhouse in Mayfair. He has presented many television series, including 'Rhodes Around Britain', 'Open Rhodes' and a children's series based on Roald Dahl's book *Revolting Recipes*. In 1996 he won the CATEY Special Award at the *Hotel & Caterer Magazine* Awards for his contribution to the British food industry. Gary teamed up with Sodexho Alliance in 1997 to open City Rhodes, within 10 months achieving a Michelin star, and Rhodes in the Square. More restaurants are planned. Gary continues the training principles of Master Class by giving Sodexho Alliance chefs an opportunity to train within the restaurant kitchens.

Gary Rhodes

Gary Rhodes

cooks at Murrayfield Stadium, Edinburgh

"Master Class is an opportunity for me to inspire fellow chefs and help them understand the importance of balancing taste, texture and flavour."

menu
serves 6

Watercress, spinach and
  Parmesan salad with cider
  vinegar and mustard dressing

Escalope of salmon with
  black treacle, juniper and
  sherry dressing

Roast chumps of lamb with spring
  greens and pickled red onions

Chocolate banana bread pudding
  with chocolate sorbet

wine suggestions

Bouché Père et Fils,
  Cuvée Réservée, Brut

Pewsey Vale Vineyard Eden
  Valley Riesling 1994

Château Lyonnat 1989/90,
  Lussac – St Émilion

Passito di Pantelleria, Pellegrino

Watercress, spinach and Parmesan salad with cider vinegar and mustard dressing

This is a very basic recipe that can have so many combinations: spring onions, garlic croûtons, French beans and lots more tastes can be added, as shown in the picture below. The cider dressing can also be used in salads of your choice. I sometimes use it to season and flavour spinach to go with pork dishes.

Gary Rhodes

ingredients

2–3 bunches of watercress (about 100 g/4 oz in total)

100 g/4 oz baby spinach leaves

100 g/4 oz fresh Parmesan cheese, flaked, or 50 g/2 oz Parmesan, freshly grated

FOR THE DRESSING:

1½ tablespoons cider vinegar

1 heaped teaspoon caster sugar

1 egg

1 egg yolk

2 teaspoons Dijon mustard

300 ml/½ pint groundnut oil

salt and freshly ground black pepper

To make the dressing, warm the cider vinegar with the sugar, then leave to cool. Mix the egg and egg yolk with the mustard and add the sugared vinegar. Whisk together, then gradually add the groundnut oil a drop at a time, whisking continuously as you would when making mayonnaise. Season with salt and pepper.

Sprinkle enough dressing over the salad leaves and Parmesan to coat them lightly (any leftover dressing can be kept in the fridge for a few days). Divide between individual plates or serve in a large bowl for everybody to help themselves.

Escalope of salmon with black treacle, juniper and sherry dressing

This dressing works well with smoked salmon, trout, mackerel or herrings, too. Pan-fried scallops sitting on the treacle dressing are also very good.

Gary Rhodes

ingredients

6 x 100–175 g/4–6 oz slices of salmon fillet, 1 cm/½ inch thick

a knob of butter

225 g/8 oz mixed green salad leaves, e.g. rocket, baby spinach

1 teaspoon olive oil, mixed with a few drops of lemon juice

salt and freshly ground black pepper

FOR THE DRESSING:

3 heaped tablespoons finely chopped shallots or onions

15–18 black peppercorns, crushed

20–30 juniper berries, finely chopped

1 large garlic clove, crushed

6 tablespoons sherry vinegar

1½ teaspoons black treacle

4½ tablespoons walnut oil

4½ tablespoons groundnut or grapeseed oil

a pinch of salt

To make the dressing, put the shallots or onions, peppercorns, juniper berries, garlic and sherry vinegar in a small pan and simmer until the vinegar has almost completely evaporated. Add the black treacle and oils and bring back to a simmer. Cook for 1–2 minutes and then season with the salt. This dressing can be made hours or even days in advance. It is best kept refrigerated – the flavours will become more dominant as it relaxes – and brought back to a warm temperature before serving.

To cook the salmon, first heat a frying pan and season the salmon with salt and pepper. Add the butter to the pan and lay the salmon slices, presentation-side down, in the sizzling butter. Cook for 2–3 minutes on one side only, keeping the fish pink. While the salmon is cooking, spoon the dressing on to 4 serving plates. Season the green leaves and toss with the olive oil and lemon juice. Sit them on top of the dressing. Place the salmon, presentation-side up, on top of the leaves. The dish is now ready to serve.

Roast chumps of lamb with spring greens and pickled red onions

Chumps of lamb are normally sold as chump chops. These aren't; they are the chump joint taken off the bone, the same place the chops come from (rear end of the saddle), but to be served as individual portion roasts. They need trimming of some fat and tidying up, then you have a wonderful portion of lamb with just a little fat covering and ready for roasting. A good idea is to reheat the pickled red onions in the roasting tin for the last 10 minutes so that they absorb the wonderful flavours of the roast itself.

Gary Rhodes

ingredients

6 lamb chumps, trimmed

1 kg/2¼ lb spring greens, stalks removed, cut into strips 1 cm/½ inch wide

a large knob of unsalted butter

salt and freshly ground black pepper

FOR THE PICKLED RED ONIONS:

700 g/1½ lb red onions, unpeeled

150 ml/¼ pint olive oil

150 ml/¼ pint groundnut oil

150 ml/¼ pint balsamic vinegar

a squeeze of lemon juice

The red onions can be prepared well in advance. Cut each onion into 6 or 8 wedges, making sure the core is kept intact as this holds the onions together. Bring a pan of water to the boil, add the onions and cook for 1–2 minutes. Warm together the oils, balsamic vinegar and lemon juice. When the onions are ready, drain them and add to the oil and vinegar mix, keeping them off the heat. Season with salt and pepper. The onions are now marinating and should be turned over occasionally to ensure even flavouring. It's best to make them at least 1–2 hours before eating. They should then only be served warm; if they become too hot the real flavour is lost.

Season the lamb and put it fat-side down in a roasting tin on top of the stove over a medium heat. Cook for a few minutes before turning it in the tin until each side is sealed and browned, then transfer to an oven preheated to 200°C/400°F/Gas Mark 6 and roast for 12–15 minutes for a pink finish, depending on the size of the cut. It's very important to give chumps of lamb a good 8–10 minutes' resting time once cooked, to relax the meat.

While the lamb is resting, blanch the spring greens in boiling salted water for ½–1 minute, then drain. Add a knob of butter and season with salt and pepper.

To serve, reheat the onions until just warm. Spoon the greens at 6 o'clock on each serving plate with the red onions and some of the marinade at 12 o'clock. Now all we need to do is carve the chumps of lamb and sit them on top of the greens.

Chocolate banana bread pudding with chocolate sorbet

This pudding will fulfil all chocolate lovers' fantasies! Imagine a rich chocolate and banana cake filled with melting chocolate ganache. And then imagine a chocolate sauce and chocolate sorbet to go with it. The beauty of this recipe is that it can be made well in advance and then microwaved, which not only heats the cake but also starts the chocolate melting inside.

You could use a bought banana loaf instead of making your own. In fact you needn't stick to banana bread – a golden syrup or Jamaican gingerbread loaf will also work very well or, if you're the ultimate chocolate freak, you could always use a chocolate cake!

Clotted cream, placed on top of the cake, eats very well with this dish.

ingredients

FOR THE BANANA BREAD:

125 g/4½ oz butter

100 g/4 oz soft light brown sugar

100 g/4 oz granulated sugar

2 medium eggs

250 g/9 oz very ripe bananas, mashed

325 g/11 oz plain flour

1 teaspoon baking powder

a good pinch of salt

FOR THE CHOCOLATE SORBET:

150 g/5 oz good-quality plain chocolate, broken into pieces

500 ml/17 fl oz water

150 g/5 oz caster sugar

25 g/1 oz glucose syrup

First make the banana bread. Butter a 900 g/2 lb loaf tin and line it with greaseproof paper. Cream the butter with the soft light brown and granulated sugars. Beat the eggs together and add slowly to the butter mix. Mix the mashed bananas into the butter mixture. Sift together the flour, baking powder and salt and fold into the banana-butter mix. Spoon the mixture into the lined tin and bake in an oven preheated to 180°C/350°F/Gas Mark 4 for 50–60 minutes. Leave to cool for 10–15 minutes before turning out of the tin. Once the loaf is cold, cut off all the crust, then cut the bread into 1 cm/ ½ inch dice. Set aside, ready to be soaked with the chocolate custard.

Next make the chocolate sorbet. Put the chocolate pieces in a bowl. Bring the water, sugar and glucose to the boil and pour on to the chocolate pieces. Stir until the chocolate has melted. Leave to cool and then chill. The sorbet mix is now ready to churn in an ice-cream maker, which should take about 20–25 minutes. Transfer the sorbet to a box, cover and place into the freezer. If you do not have an ice-cream machine, simply freeze the mixture, whisking it occasionally as it hardens to help create a smooth consistency.

/continued...

FOR THE CHOCOLATE GANACHE:

125 g/4½ oz good-quality plain chocolate, broken into small pieces

15 g/½ oz butter, diced

190 ml/6½ fl oz double cream

2 tablespoons granulated sugar

FOR THE CHOCOLATE TUILE BISCUITS:

(makes about 10–12)

15 g/½ oz cocoa powder

50 g/2 oz icing sugar

50 g/2 oz plain flour

1 egg white

50 g/2 oz butter, melted

For the chocolate ganache, put the chocolate and butter in a bowl. Bring the double cream to the boil with the granulated sugar, then pour it over the chocolate and butter and mix well until melted. Leave to cool, then chill until set. Once set and firm, roll the ganache into balls approximately 2.5 cm/1 inch in diameter and then chill until needed. These ganache balls will be placed in the centre of the cakes, creating the melted chocolate filling.

Now make the chocolate tuiles. You will need a large baking sheet covered with baking parchment to spread the biscuits on and a stencil to shape them, which could be a triangle, leaf shape, circle, etc. I prefer to use a plastic lid with a circle 7.5–10 cm/3–4 inches in diameter cut out of it. This gives you a permanent stencil to wash and use time and time again.

Sift together the cocoa powder, icing sugar and flour. Slowly mix in the egg white, then the melted butter. Place the stencil on the baking parchment. Spread enough of the mixture inside it to give a thin shape. Lift and repeat the stencil shapes. Bake in an oven preheated to 160°C/325°F/Gas Mark 3 for 5–6 minutes. Once they are cooked and while still warm, lift the biscuits off the paper with a palette knife and drape them over upturned cups or small bowls to give you a biscuit-cup shape to sit the sorbet in. You could also cut a cardboard cylinder (from the centre of a roll of foil or clingfilm) in half lengthways. Push a tuile into it, which will give you a curved biscuit once it has cooled. The cooked tuile biscuits will keep for 48 hours in an airtight container.

FOR THE CHOCOLATE CUSTARD:

175 ml/6 fl oz double cream

575 ml/19 fl oz milk

65 g/2½ oz butter, diced

250 g/9 oz good-quality plain chocolate, broken into small pieces

3 eggs

2 egg yolks

150 g/5 oz soft brown sugar

FOR THE ULTIMATE CHOCOLATE SAUCE:

225 g/8 oz good-quality plain chocolate

250 ml/8 fl oz double cream

25 g/1 oz unsalted butter

To make the chocolate custard, bring the cream and milk to the boil in a saucepan. Put the butter and chocolate in a bowl, pour on the cream mixture and stir, melting the two together. Whisk together the eggs, egg yolks and sugar. Pour the chocolate cream on to the eggs and then strain through a sieve. Pour the chocolate custard over the diced banana bread, mixing it in well to help the banana bread soak up the chocolate flavour. Leave to soak for 30 minutes.

To make the chocolate sauce, melt the chocolate with the cream in a bowl set over a pan of hot water and, once warm, add the butter. You now have a thick, rich chocolate sauce. This is best eaten cold or just warm. Trying to serve this as a hot sauce will simply cause the butter to separate.

To finish the dish, butter 6 pastry rings, 7.5 cm/3 inches in diameter and 5 cm/2 inches deep. Put them on a baking sheet lined with greased greaseproof paper or baking parchment. Spoon a layer of the soaked cake into the moulds and put a ball of ganache in the centre. Continue to fill the moulds with care until the ganache ball is covered. Bake the puddings in an oven preheated to 160°C/325°F/Gas Mark 3 for 10–15 minutes. During the baking, the chocolate custard and banana cake mixture will set and give a baked-cake finish with melting ganache inside. Leave the puddings to cool or serve immediately. The advantage of this dessert is that these puddings can be left to cool and then refrigerated. To serve, they then simply need to be microwaved.

To finish the presentation, thread some of the chocolate sauce across each plate and sit the warm pudding on top. Next to the pudding, put a tuile biscuit and, using a dessertspoon or an ice-cream scoop, fill with the chocolate sorbet.

The pudding is now complete and ready to eat!

Rick Stein was brought up in Oxfordshire and spent two years travelling the world before returning to study English at Oxford University. In 1975 he opened The Seafood Restaurant in Padstow, Cornwall, which has gained a reputation as the finest fish restaurant in the country. Rick Stein is renowned for his passionate espousal of fish cookery – both at the restaurant, in two BBC television series and in his cookery books. *English Seafood Cookery* won the Glenfiddich Award for Food Book of the Year in 1979. This was followed by *Taste of the Sea*, which won the 1995 André Simon Memorial Fund Food Book Award. The Gardner Merchant Master Class at Blenheim formed part of his BBC series 'Fruits of the Sea', which was accompanied by a book of the same name.

Rick Stein

Rick Stein
cooks at
Blenheim Palace

"As we entered the grounds of Blenheim Palace I suddenly realized how far from Padstow I was. I always think of these events as 'playing away from home'."

menu

serves 4

Carpetshell clams with aïoli

Panaché of scallops, squid and
John Dory with a tomato,
tarragon and chervil dressing

Sliced crayfish served with a
vanilla sauce

Fresh raspberries with panna cotta

wine suggestions

Tavel Rosé 1994 Château d'Aquéria

Riesling 1994, Cave Vinicole de
Ribeauvillé

St Aubin 1988, Louis Jadot

Passito di Pantelleria 1993,
Carlo Pellegrino

Carpetshell clams with aïoli

If you can't get any live clams for this dish, do try it with small mussels instead.

To make the aïoli, mix the egg yolk, vinegar and salt together in a bowl, then place the bowl on a tea towel to stop it slipping. Using a wire whisk, beat the oil into the egg mixture a few drops at a time until you have incorporated it all. Once you have carefully added about the same volume of oil as the original mixture of egg yolks and vinegar, you can add the oil more quickly. Mix in the garlic and set aside.

Scrub the clams with a stiff brush to remove any sand or dirt, then wash in plenty of cold water. Put the clams in a large pan with the white wine, then cover and cook over a high heat, shaking the pan occasionally, for 2–3 minutes, until they have opened. Discard any clams that remain closed. Take the pan off the heat and stir in the aïoli and chopped parsley. Serve hot, with lots of crusty French bread.

Rick Stein

ingredients

900 g/2 lb carpetshell clams

60 ml/2 fl oz dry white wine

1 tablespoon finely chopped fresh parsley

FOR THE AÏOLI:

1 egg yolk

1 teaspoon white wine vinegar

¼ teaspoon salt

150 ml/¼ pint olive oil

5 garlic cloves, very finely chopped

Panaché of scallops, squid and John Dory with a tomato, tarragon and chervil dressing

Rick Stein

ingredients

175 g/6 oz cleaned squid, thinly sliced

a little paprika

a little olive oil for frying the squid

8 fresh scallops, each cut into 2 discs

a little butter for frying the scallops

225 g/8 oz John Dory fillet, skinned and cut into slices 2.5 cm/1 inch thick

15 g/½ oz lamb's lettuce

1 teaspoon lemon olive oil

a little finely grated lemon zest

salt and freshly ground black pepper

FOR THE DRESSING:

60 ml/2 fl oz olive oil

1 tablespoon clarified butter (see page 146)

25 g/1 oz peeled, deseeded tomato, diced

30 ml/1 fl oz very well reduced fish stock

1 small garlic clove, very finely chopped

1 teaspoon roughly chopped fresh tarragon

1 teaspoon roughly chopped fresh chervil

¼ teaspoon finger chillies, deseeded and finely chopped

1 tablespoon white wine vinegar

a pinch of saffron strands

½ teaspoon finely chopped anchovies

Put all the ingredients for the dressing in a saucepan and gently warm through. Do not bring it anywhere near boiling. Season with salt and pepper to taste.

Sprinkle the squid with a little paprika and fry briefly in a little olive oil over a high heat until lightly browned. In a separate pan, briefly fry the scallops in a tiny amount of butter over a high heat until browned. Season both with salt and pepper. Season the John Dory with salt only and steam briefly until opaque.

Toss the lamb's lettuce in the lemon oil and sprinkle with the lemon zest. To serve, pile the seafood just off centre on 4 warmed plates and surround with the dressing. Place a pile of salad leaves next to the fish.

Sliced crayfish served with a vanilla sauce

Rick Stein

ingredients

1 live crayfish (spiny lobster), weighing about 1.5–1.75 kg (3½–4 lb), or 2 live lobsters, weighing about 700 g–1 kg (1½–2¼ lb) each

FOR THE VANILLA SAUCE:

½ vanilla pod

300 ml/½ pint fish stock

2 tablespoons Noilly Prat

2 tablespoons water

2 egg yolks

225 g/8 oz unsalted butter, clarified (see below) and kept warm

juice of 1 lemon

a good pinch of cayenne pepper

½ teaspoon salt

freshly ground black pepper

Put the lobster in the freezer for 2 hours. Remove and cook in a very large pan of boiling salted water for 25 minutes if you are using 1 large crayfish or 15–20 minutes for smaller lobsters. Leave to cool, then remove the meat. To do this, detach the head from the tail, cut the head in half and remove the soft, greenish tomalley (liver) and the roe. Turn the tail section over and cut along either side of the flat under-shell with scissors. Lift back the flap and take out the meat in one piece. Slice on a slant into pieces 1 cm/½ inch thick, removing the intestinal tract from the centre of each slice with the point of a sharp knife.

For the sauce, split the vanilla pod open lengthways and scrape out the seeds. Put the fish stock, vanilla pod and seeds and Noilly Prat into a pan and boil rapidly until reduced to about 1½–2 tablespoons. Remove the pan from the heat; discard the vanilla pod.

Put the water and egg yolks in a bowl set over a pan of simmering water, making sure the base of the bowl is not touching the water. Whisk until voluminous and creamy. Remove the bowl from the pan and whisk in the reduced fish stock. Then gradually whisk in the warm clarified butter, building up an emulsion. Add the lemon juice, cayenne pepper, salt and black pepper. (Alternatively you can make the sauce in a blender: put the egg yolks, lemon juice and water into the blender, turn on and pour in the reduced fish stock, followed by the clarified butter. Season with the cayenne, salt and black pepper.)

To serve, heat the lobster gently and arrange the slices of tail meat on 4 warmed plates. Put a little pile of the warmed head meat to one side and a spoonful of the vanilla sauce to the other.

TO CLARIFY BUTTER

Melt the butter in a pan over a low heat, then skim off any froth from the surface. Pour off the clear butter into another pan, leaving behind the white solids that will have collected at the bottom.

Fresh raspberries with panna cotta

This Italian light set cream can be served with stewed rhubarb in winter and with whatever fresh berries you like in summer but I always favour raspberries.

ingredients

300 ml/½ pint double cream

300 ml/½ pint milk

6 tablespoons caster sugar

1 vanilla pod

2 teaspoons powdered gelatine

a few fresh raspberries and fresh mint sprigs, to decorate

FOR THE RASPBERRY SAUCE:

250 g/9 oz fresh raspberries

50 g/2 oz caster sugar

juice of ½ lemon

Put the cream, milk, sugar and vanilla pod into a small pan and simmer gently for 5 minutes, then remove from the heat. Meanwhile, put 2 tablespoons of cold water in a small pan and sprinkle the gelatine over it. Set aside for 5 minutes, then heat gently until clear.

Remove the vanilla pod from the cream and stir in the dissolved gelatine. Strain the mixture and pour into 4 dariole moulds or ramekins, cover and chill for 3 hours or until set.

To make the sauce, purée the raspberries with the sugar and lemon juice, then pass through a fine sieve.

To serve, unmould the panna cotta on to serving plates and pour the sauce around, then garnish with fresh raspberries and sprigs of mint.

Franco Taruschio was born in Montefano, Italy, and trained as a hotelier in Italy, Switzerland and France before coming to the UK in 1961 to learn English. In 1963 he bought The Walnut Tree Inn, a rural pub in South Wales, with his English wife, Ann. At first they struggled to make a living, their Italian-influenced food greeted with some suspicion by the inn's regulars. But gradually word spread, and The Walnut Tree Inn is now one of Britain's most admired restaurants. Franco loves to cook the food of his native Marche region but his menus are also shaped by influences as diverse as Thai, Eastern European and Spanish. With his wife he has written *Leaves from The Walnut Tree, Bruschetta, Crostoni and* Crostini, and *Franco and Friends*, that accompanied the BBC series of the same name.

Franco Taruschio

Franco Taruschio
cooks at The National Museum of Wales

"I included appetizers and a trio of desserts to ensure that the chefs had lots to learn, and that the meal would be memorable for everyone who attended."

menu
serves 4

Appetizers
Crescente
Glamorgan sausages
A selection of stuffed olives

Cod with rösti and caponata
  marchigiani

Roast best end of lamb with
  wild mushrooms
Baked polenta with ricotta

Trio of puddings
Tiramisù
Chocolate brandy loaf
Pasta torte

wine suggestions

Prosecco, Brut, Collavini with fresh peach

Sancerre, Les Collinettes 1993/94

Château Peymartin 1990

Bodenham Seyve Villard 1990

Crescente

ingredients

500 g/1 lb 2 oz type '0' flour
(available from Italian delicatessens)

1 teaspoon salt

a good pinch of bicarbonate of soda

about 300 ml/½ pint milk

extra virgin olive oil

sea salt

TOPPINGS (SELECT FROM THE FOLLOWING):

roasted cherry tomatoes • salami • fresh basil leaves • rocket • pesto sauce • anchovy curls • Parma ham curls • mozzarella slices • shavings of Parmesan cheese

This dough does not have to be used all at once as it will keep for 2 days.

Knead the flour, salt, bicarbonate of soda and milk together to make a dough. Wrap the dough in a cloth and leave to rest in the refrigerator for 1 hour.

Break off pieces of dough the size of a marble and roll out into discs about 5 cm/2 inches in diameter.

Heat a little extra virgin olive oil in a heavy-based non-stick frying pan. Fry the discs, a few at a time, until golden on both sides; they will bubble all over. Change the olive oil in the pan 2 or 3 times. Drain on kitchen paper, sprinkle with sea salt and serve at once, with a selection of the toppings.

152

Franco Taruschio

Glamorgan sausages

ingredients

285 g/10 oz Caerphilly cheese, grated

225 g/8 oz white breadcrumbs, made from day-old bread

4 tablespoons finely chopped spring onions

2 large egg yolks

2 heaped tablespoons finely chopped fresh parsley

1 teaspoon fresh thyme

2 teaspoons English mustard powder

vegetable oil for deep-frying

salt and freshly ground black pepper

FOR COATING:

plain flour

2 large egg whites

crisp dried breadcrumbs

Mix together all the ingredients except the oil and shape into sausages the size of a little finger. Coat the sausages first lightly in flour, then in the egg white and finally in dried breadcrumbs. Chill for half an hour, then deep-fry in hot oil until golden. Drain on kitchen paper and serve immediately.

Cod with rösti and caponata marchigiani

Franco Taruschio

ingredients

400 g/14 oz aubergines

40 g/1½ oz pine nuts

175 ml/6 fl oz extra virgin olive oil

800 g/1¾ lb cod (or turbot) fillet, skinned

600 g/1¼ lb potatoes

300 g/10½ oz plum tomatoes, peeled, deseeded and cut into 1 cm/½ inch dice

25 large fresh basil leaves, shredded (use your fingers; a knife would discolour the basil)

1 lemon, cut into 4 wedges

salt and freshly ground black pepper

Cut the aubergines into quarters, then remove and discard the flesh containing the seeds. Cut the aubergines into 1 cm/½ inch dice. Sprinkle with salt, leave in a colander for 30 minutes to drain, then pat dry.

Fry the pine nuts in 1 tablespoon of the oil until light golden, then drain on kitchen paper and set aside.

Cut the fish into 8 equal pieces, season with salt and pepper and set aside.

Peel the potatoes and shred them into matchstick pieces on a mandoline or, failing this, a cheese grater. Do not rinse them as this will wash away the starch. Heat 75 ml/2½ fl oz of the oil in a large non-stick ovenproof frying pan. Spread half the shredded potato over the top of the fish pieces. When the oil is hot, put the fish in it potato-side down, using 2 fish slices. Cook until the potato is deep golden, then spread the remaining potato evenly over the top of the fish. Turn the fish over and cook until deep golden. If the fish is thick, put the frying pan in a hot oven for about a minute to ensure that the fish is cooked through.

While the fish is cooking, make the caponata: heat the remaining oil in a separate frying pan until smoking. Add the aubergine and cook stirring constantly, until sealed on all sides. Stir in the tomatoes, pine nuts and basil and cook, stirring all the time, for about a minute, until the tomatoes are heated through. Taste and check the seasoning.

Mound the caponata up on 4 plates and gently overlap 2 pieces of fish on one side of each mound. Serve with the lemon wedges.

Roast best end of lamb with wild mushrooms

ingredients

4 best ends of young Welsh lamb, each with 6 bones

2 tablespoons olive oil

100 g/4 oz fresh breadcrumbs

1 teaspoon each of chopped fresh thyme, parsley and marjoram

2 eggs, beaten

225 g/8 oz mixed wild mushrooms, such as ceps, chanterelles, oyster mushrooms, pieds de mouton, trompettes de mort

2 tablespoons extra virgin olive oil

salt and freshly ground black pepper

FOR THE SAUCE:

1 large onion, roughly chopped

2 carrots, chopped

3 celery sticks, chopped

2 bay leaves

125 ml/4 fl oz Marsala

1 tablespoon tomato purée

6 garlic cloves, crushed

1 fresh rosemary sprig

Trim the lamb, removing all the fat and cleaning the bones up to the eye of the meat. Set aside in a cold place while you prepare the sauce.

For the sauce, brown the trimmings from the lamb in a roasting tin, then pour off all the surplus fat and transfer the remainder to a saucepan. Add the onion, carrots, celery and bay leaves to the roasting tin and brown well over a high heat or in the oven. Add the Marsala to the tin and bring to the boil, scraping to incorporate all the cooking juices. Stir in the tomato purée and 900 ml/ 1½ pints of water, then transfer the contents of the roasting tin to the saucepan. Add the garlic and rosemary, bring to the boil, then lower the heat and simmer for 1½ hours, skimming constantly. Push the contents of the pan through a fine sieve and boil until reduced to the consistency of single cream. Keep the sauce warm until needed.

Heat the olive oil in a frying pan and seal the lamb all over. Remove from the pan.

Mix the breadcrumbs with the chopped herbs and season with salt and pepper. Brush the surface of the lamb with the beaten egg, then press a layer of breadcrumbs over the meat to make a crust. Roast the lamb in an oven preheated to 190°C/375°F/Gas Mark 5 for about 7 minutes or until it is cooked but still pink. Remove the meat from the oven and allow it to rest for 4 minutes.

Fry the mushrooms in the extra virgin olive oil and season to taste.

Carve the lamb into double chops, removing one bone. Serve with the sauce, wild mushrooms and Baked polenta with ricotta (see page 157).

Franco Taruschio

Baked polenta with ricotta

Instant polenta flour is available, which only needs cooking for a few minutes. It is not quite as good as the original method but is not a bad substitute if you are pressed for time.

ingredients

300 g/10½ oz onion, finely chopped
50 g/2 oz butter
freshly grated nutmeg
350 ml/12 fl oz milk
600 g/1¼ lb fresh ricotta cheese
freshly grated Parmesan cheese
salt and freshly ground
black pepper

FOR THE POLENTA:
900 ml/1½ pints water
300 g/10½ oz polenta flour
olive oil

First prepare the polenta: put the water in a large pan with some salt and bring to the boil. Add the polenta flour to the boiling water, letting it drop in like sand sifting through your fingers. As the flour is falling into the water, stir with a wooden spoon. Always stir in one direction, never change direction. Keep stirring for 30–40 minutes. You should end up with a fairly thick paste, but not too thick to pour.

Pour the polenta on to a lightly oiled tin in a layer 2.5 cm/1 inch thick and leave until cold.

Meanwhile, gently fry the onion in the butter until golden, then season with salt, pepper and a pinch of nutmeg. Add the milk and cook over a low heat for half an hour.

Lightly butter a gratin dish. Thinly slice the polenta and put a layer in the dish. Scatter over some ricotta and spread over a little of the onion sauce, then top with a sprinkling of grated Parmesan. Continue layering in this way, finishing with the onion sauce and a lot of Parmesan. Place in an oven preheated to 220°C/425°F/ Gas Mark 7 and bake until the top is golden.

Franco Taruschio

Tiramisù

ingredients

1 egg

50 g/2 oz caster sugar

250 g/9 oz mascarpone cheese

150 ml/¼ pint whipping cream

3 tablespoons rum

3 tablespoons Tia Maria

3 tablespoons brandy

150 ml/¼ pint strong black coffee, preferably espresso

16 boudoir biscuits

cocoa powder for dusting

Put the egg and sugar in a bowl and whisk until thick and pale. Add the mascarpone and whisk for a further minute. In a separate bowl, whip the cream until thickened. Fold it into the egg and mascarpone mixture.

Line a 450 g/1 lb loaf tin (about 600 ml/1 pint in capacity) with clingfilm. Mix together the rum, Tia Maria, brandy and coffee. Spread a thin layer of the cream mixture over the base of the tin. Dip half the boudoir biscuits into the coffee mixture one by one and arrange them in a layer on top of the cream. Spread another layer of cream on top, thickly this time, followed by the remaining biscuits, dipped as before. Finish with a layer of cream. Dust the top with cocoa powder, then leave in the fridge until required.

To serve, turn out of the tin and peel off the clingfilm, then dust with cocoa powder and cut into slices.

Chocolate brandy loaf

ingredients

125 g/4½ oz butter

100 g/4 oz caster sugar

2 egg yolks

90 ml/3 fl oz strong black coffee

14 boudoir biscuits

2 tablespoons brandy

75 g/3 oz plain or bitter chocolate, chopped into small pieces

75 g/3 oz flaked almonds, toasted

12 amaretti biscuit halves

2 tablespoons rum

2 tablespoons Tia Maria

Beat the butter and sugar together until creamy. Beat the egg yolks until pale, add them to the butter mixture and continue beating until the mixture is creamy. Slowly add the coffee, beating until it has all been amalgamated. Divide the mixture into three.

Dip 7 boudoir biscuits in the brandy and put them on a tray or a flat plate. Cover with one third of the coffee mixture. Sprinkle with one third of the chopped chocolate and flaked almonds. Dip the amaretti biscuits in the rum and place on top of the chocolate and nut layer. Put a second layer of coffee mixture on top and sprinkle with half the remaining chocolate and nuts. Dip the remaining 7 boudoir biscuits in the Tia Maria and place on top.

Cover the top with the last portion of coffee mixture. Scatter the remaining chocolate and nuts on top and chill for 48 hours before serving.

Pasta torte

ingredients

finely grated rind and juice of 2 oranges

finely grated rind and juice of 1 lemon

5 egg yolks

125 g/4½ oz caster sugar

100 g/4 oz dried tagliatelle

4 tablespoons clear honey

FOR THE PASTRY:

175 g/6 oz plain flour

½ tablespoon caster sugar

90 g/3¼ oz butter

1 egg yolk

To make the pastry, sift the flour and sugar into a bowl and rub in the butter until the mixture resembles breadcrumbs. Beat the egg yolk with a little chilled water, sprinkle it over the dough and work in lightly with your fingertips. Cover and chill for half an hour. Roll out and use to line a 17.5 cm/7 inch flan tin.

Mix together the orange and lemon rinds and juice. Beat the egg yolks with the sugar until creamy and add to the juice and rind. Pour into the pastry case and bake in an oven preheated to 150°C/300°F/Gas Mark 2 for 40 minutes. Cook the tagliatelle in boiling, salted water until *al dente*, then drain well and toss with the honey. Pile it on top of the hot tart and return to the oven for 7–8 minutes, until the pasta is crisp and golden. Serve hot.

Franco Taruschio

Antony Worrall Thompson worked in a succession of London restaurants before opening the fashionable Ménage à Trois in Knightsbridge in 1981, which won fame for its innovative menu composed of just starters and puddings. He has taken consultancies for a number of companies with whom he has launched restaurants such as dell'Ugo, Zoë and Palio. In 1997 he set up his own restaurant, Woz, in London. Winner of numerous culinary awards, Antony Worrall Thompson

Antony Worrall Thompson

Antony Worrall Thompson
cooks at Wilton Castle

"I wanted to produce hearty, wholesome food that would be easy to eat, creating a relaxed, fun dining experience."

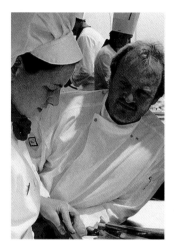

menu

serves 4

Fresh pears with Stilton
  and watercress

Mollet eggs with smoked
  salmon and cod's roe

Lamb shanks with garlic,
  rosemary and butterbeans
Roasted vegetables
Colcannon

Trio of crème brûlée

wine suggestions

Sandy Ridge Sauvignon Blanc 1992

Beaune Clos des Ursules 1988
  Louis Jadot

Champagne de Meric Rosé

Fresh pears with Stilton and watercress

ingredients

4 ripe pears, peeled, cored and quartered

225 g/8 oz Stilton cheese

50 g/2 oz butter

150 g/5 oz Cheddar cheese, grated

6 tablespoons double cream

3 large egg yolks

1 bunch of watercress, divided into sprigs

salt and freshly ground black pepper

Place the pear quarters in 4 gratin dishes. Crumble the Stilton over them and set aside. Put the butter, Cheddar, cream and egg yolks in a non-stick saucepan and stir over a low heat until they have combined into a thick cream. Continue to cook, without boiling, until the mixture has thickened. Season to taste, then spoon the mixture over the pears and place in an oven preheated to 220°C/425°F/Gas Mark 7 until brown – about 5–10 minutes. Serve with the watercress.

Antony Worrall Thompson

Mollet eggs with smoked salmon and cod's roe

ingredients

4 large free-range eggs

100 g/4 oz Scottish smoked salmon, sliced

4 slices of wholemeal bread, buttered

100 g/4 oz smoked cod's roe

6 tablespoons double cream

lemon juice

freshly ground black pepper

dill sprigs, to garnish

Don't cook the eggs for too long – when cut open, as shown, the yolks should be still runny.

Plunge the eggs into boiling salted water and cook for 3–4 minutes, depending on their size. Place under cold water and crack them all over. When ready to serve, shell the eggs and wrap each whole egg in the smoked salmon. Cut a circle from each slice of wholemeal bread and place an egg on each circle. Beat the roe and cream together until thick, then season with a little lemon juice and black pepper. Spoon the smoked cod's roe cream over, or next to, the eggs and garnish with the dill sprigs.

Antony Worrall Thompson

Lamb shanks with garlic, rosemary and butterbeans

ingredients

4 lamb shanks

6 canned anchovies

12 small rosemary sprigs

12 slivers of garlic

salt and freshly ground
black pepper

FOR BRAISING:

50 g/2 oz duck fat, butter or dripping

4 carrots, roughly chopped

2 celery sticks, roughly chopped

2 leeks, roughly chopped

2 onions, roughly chopped

2 heads of garlic, broken up

2 fresh thyme sprigs

2 fresh rosemary sprigs

2 fresh bay leaves

1 bottle of red wine

about 300 ml/½ pint chicken or
lamb stock, or water

2.5 cm/1 inch rounds of French
bread, toasted, to garnish

FOR THE BUTTERBEAN MIXTURE:

4 tablespoons extra virgin olive oil

225 g/8 oz streaky bacon lardons
(small cubes), blanched

1 carrot, finely diced

1 celery stick, finely diced

1 onion, finely diced

12 garlic cloves, peeled
but left whole

4 fresh thyme sprigs

4 fresh rosemary sprigs, chopped

8 tomatoes, chopped

400 g/14 oz can of butterbeans

Trim most of the fat from the lamb shanks. Make 3 deep incisions in each one and insert in each half an anchovy wrapped around a sprig of rosemary and a sliver of garlic. Season the meat. Heat the duck fat, butter or dripping in a large casserole, add the lamb and fry until browned all over. Remove the meat from the pan and add the carrots, celery, leeks, onions, garlic and herbs. Cook over a high heat until the vegetables are brown. Pour in the red wine, scraping up the residue from the base of the pan to deglaze. Add the stock or water. Place the joints on top of the vegetables, then cover and cook in an oven preheated to 140–150°C/275–300°F/ Gas Mark 1–2 for 2½ hours, topping up with a little more stock or water if it gets too dry.

To make the butterbean mixture, heat the oil in a large pan and brown the bacon in it. Reduce the heat and add the carrot, celery, onion and garlic. Cook for about 8 minutes, until softened. Stir in the thyme, rosemary, tomatoes and butterbeans, then set aside.

When the lamb has finished cooking, remove the meat from the casserole and keep warm in a separate casserole. Whizz the residue of ingredients in a blender or food processor until smooth. Pass this sauce through a sieve on to the bean mixture and simmer for 30 minutes. Season to taste, then pour the mixture over the lamb and heat through in the oven for 10 minutes. Serve garnished with the toasted French bread.

166

Antony Worrall Thompson

Roasted vegetables

ingredients

2 onions, quartered

2 parsnips, quartered

2 carrots, halved

1 celeriac, quartered

2 potatoes, quartered

4 garlic cloves

a bunch of fresh rosemary

1 bay leaf

4 tablespoons olive oil

2 tablespoons balsamic vinegar

sea salt and coarsely ground black pepper

Combine all the ingredients in a baking tin and roast in an oven preheated to 200°C/400°F/Gas Mark 6 for 1 hour or until tender, stirring frequently.

Antony Worrall Thompson

Colcannon

ingredients

350 g/12 oz potatoes, peeled and chopped

350 g/12 oz cabbage or kale, chopped

2 small leeks, chopped

125 ml/4 fl oz cream

1 teaspoon salt

1 teaspoon freshly ground black pepper

a pinch of mace

100 g/4 oz unsalted butter, melted

Boil the potatoes until tender, then drain and mash well. Cook the cabbage or kale in boiling salted water until tender, then drain and mix with the mashed potatoes. Cook the leeks in the cream until tender. Fold the leeks and cream into the potato mixture with the salt, pepper and mace. Pile the mixture into a warmed dish, make a well in the centre and pour in the melted butter. Serve immediately.

Trio of crème brûlée

You will need 12 tiny ramekins for this recipe, about 90–100 ml/3–3½ fl oz in capacity.

ingredients

4 large egg yolks

50 g/2 oz caster sugar, plus extra for sprinkling

600 ml/1 pint double cream

FOR THE RHUBARB MIX:

225 g/8 oz rhubarb, cut into pieces 2.5 cm/1 inch long

1½ tablespoons orange juice

40 g/1½ oz caster sugar

grated zest of ¼ orange

grated zest of ¼ lemon

1½ teaspoons finely diced stem ginger

FOR THE GOOSEBERRY MIX:

25 g/1 oz butter

75 g/3 oz caster sugar

225 g/8 oz young green gooseberries, topped and tailed

FOR THE APPLE MIX:

225 g/8 oz Bramley apples, peeled, cored and sliced

2 tablespoons water

50 g/2 oz caster sugar

1 clove

¼ teaspoon mixed spice

¼ teaspoon mixed grated orange and lemon zest

First prepare the fruit mixes. For the rhubarb, place all the ingredients in a heavy-based pan and cook over a gentle heat until the rhubarb is soft but not mushy.

For the gooseberries, melt the butter and sugar in a large pan, add the gooseberries, then cover and cook gently for about 5 minutes. When the fruit looks yellow and has softened, remove the pan from the heat and crush the fruit with a wooden spoon, then a fork. Do not produce a purée – it should be more of a mash.

For the apple, place all the ingredients in a heavy-based pan and cook over a gentle heat until the apples are soft. Do not purée; try to keep the apples in individual pieces. Remove the clove.

To make the crème brûlée, beat the egg yolks thoroughly in a large bowl with the sugar. Bring the cream to the boil and boil for about 30 seconds. Pour immediately on to the egg yolk mixture and whisk together. Return the mixture to the pan and cook very gently, stirring constantly with a wooden spoon, until it thickens enough to coat the back of the spoon. Do not let it boil or it will curdle. Strain through a fine sieve and leave to cool.

Put a dessertspoon of the rhubarb mix in 4 ramekins, a dessertspoon of the gooseberry mix in the next 4 ramekins, and the apple mix in the final 4. Pour in the cream mixture and chill overnight.

About 2 hours before the meal, sprinkle the cream with an even layer of caster sugar about 5 mm/¼ inch thick and place under a grill preheated to maximum. The sugar will caramelize to a sheet of brown smoothness: it may be necessary to turn the dishes about to achieve an even effect. Serve each person with 3 ramekins, one of each flavour (it might be a good idea to mark the dishes underneath so you know which fruit they contain!).

Antony Worrall Thompson

A selection of festive recipes

Starters
Canapés Savoy
  Anton Edelmann

Ceviche of monkfish with avocado
  Rick Stein

Thai crispy prawn coconut treats
  Ken Hom

Main courses
Roast pheasant with
  cotechino stuffing
  Antony Worrall Thompson

Roast guinea fowl with thyme,
  wild mushrooms and garlic
  bubble and squeak
  Paul and Jeanne Rankin

Tournedos of pork with mashed potato
sauce and caramelized apple
  Gary Rhodes

Timpano di lasagne al duca d'este
  Timpano of lasagne with fillets of
  sole and shrimps
  Franco Taruschio

Shorvedar khumbi
  Mushroom curry
  Madhur Jaffrey

Puddings
Cranberry and baked pear pancakes
  with Calvados cream
  Willi Elsener

Torta di cioccolata
  Chocolate torte
  Alastair Little

Baked Christmas Alaska
  Paul Heathcote

Christmas

Canapés Savoy

Makes 40

ingredients

150 g/5 oz beef fillet

150 g/5 oz foie gras

150 g/5 oz skinless salmon fillet

5 large scallops, without roe

40 thin slices of baguette

8 tablespoons tomato ketchup

4 teaspoons freshly grated
horseradish

50 g/2 oz unsalted butter

salt and freshly ground
black pepper

Cut the beef, foie gras and salmon into 10 even-sized pieces each, to fit the bread slices. Cut each scallop horizontally in half.

Toast the bread lightly on both sides and keep warm. Place the tomato ketchup and horseradish in a small saucepan and heat gently. Spread a little on each piece of toasted bread.

Season the beef and fish with salt and pepper. Melt a third of the butter in a frying pan and fry the beef and foie gras quickly on both sides, ensuring that they remain rare. Melt the remaining butter in another frying pan and fry the salmon and scallops very quickly on both sides.

Place a piece of meat or fish on each slice of toasted bread and serve at once.

Ceviche of monkfish with avocado

Try to use monkfish fillets that have been taken from a small fish. The finished slices need to be about 4 cm/1½ inches across.

Serves 4

ingredients

350 g/12 oz monkfish fillet

juice of 2 limes

1 red finger chilli, halved and deseeded

1 small red onion, peeled

4 salad tomatoes

2 tablespoons extra virgin olive oil

1 tablespoon chopped fresh coriander, plus a little extra to garnish

1 large, ripe but firm avocado

salt

Trim any membrane from the outside of the monkfish and discard. Cut across the fillet into thin, disc-like slices and place them in a large, shallow dish. Pour over the lime juice, cover and chill for 3 hours, during which time the fish will 'cook' in the juice and turn opaque.

Meanwhile, cut across each red chilli half so that you get very thin, slightly curved slices. Cut the onion into thin wedges from the top down through the root end and then separate each wedge into individual pieces. Cover the tomatoes with boiling water and leave for 30 seconds. Drain, cover with cold water and, when they are cool enough to handle, peel off the skin. Quarter and deseed the tomatoes, then cut each quarter into thin, arc-shaped slices.

Just before you are ready to serve, lift the monkfish out of any excess lime juice and place in a bowl with the chilli, red onion, tomato, olive oil, chopped coriander and a little salt. Toss together lightly. Halve, stone and peel the avocado. Slice each half across into semi-circular slices. Arrange about 3–4 slices of avocado slightly to one side of each serving plate. Pile the ceviche to the other side and sprinkle with a little more coriander. Serve straight away, while it is still chilled.

Rick Stein Christmas

Thai crispy prawn coconut treats

Here is a simple Thai appetizer which would be quite Chinese but for the added twist of coconut and curry paste. These touches turn the dish into a wonderful party treat or a splendid opener for any dinner. The filling can be made ahead of time but the actual stuffing should be done at the last moment, otherwise the wonton skins will become soggy. These treats should not be frozen.

Serves 4

ingredients

250 g/9 oz wonton skins

600 ml/1 pint groundnut or vegetable oil, for deep-frying

FOR THE FILLING:

350 g/12 oz raw prawns, peeled and coarsely minced

100 g/4 oz minced pork

1 teaspoon salt

½ teaspoon freshly ground black pepper

4 tablespoons finely chopped spring onions

3 tablespoons desiccated coconut

2 teaspoons light soy sauce

2 tablespoons oyster sauce

1½ tablespoons finely chopped orange zest

1 teaspoon Madras curry paste

1 teaspoon sugar

Start by making the filling. Put the prawns and pork in a large bowl, add the salt and pepper and mix well, either by kneading with your hands or by stirring with a wooden spoon. Then add the rest of the filling ingredients and stir them well into the prawn and pork mixture. Cover the bowl with clingfilm and chill for at least 20 minutes.

When you are ready to stuff the parcels, put 1 tablespoon of the filling in the centre of each wonton skin. Dampen the edges with a little water and bring up the sides of the skin around the filling. Pinch the edges together at the top so that the wonton is sealed; it should look like a small filled bag.

Heat a wok or large frying pan over a high heat until it is hot. Add the oil and, when it is very hot and slightly smoking, add a handful of wontons. Fry for 3 minutes, until golden and crisp. If the oil gets too hot, turn the heat down slightly. Drain the wontons well on kitchen paper. Continue to fry the remaining wontons, then serve immediately.

Roast pheasant with cotechino stuffing

Serves 6

ingredients

3 pheasants, oven-ready

6 slices of Parma ham

6 tablespoons olive oil

3 garlic cloves, finely chopped

1 onion, finely diced

1 teaspoon soft fresh thyme leaves

100 g/4 oz chicken livers, chopped

100 g/4 oz dried porcini mushrooms, soaked for 30 minutes, drained, squeezed and chopped (reserve the soaking liquid)

350 ml/12 fl oz dry red wine

a little butter

salt and freshly ground black pepper

FOR THE STUFFING:

3 tablespoons good olive oil

2 small red onions, finely chopped

2 garlic cloves, finely chopped

2 celery sticks, finely chopped

1 carrot, finely chopped

½ teaspoon soft fresh thyme leaves

1 cotechino sausage, casing removed (Italian sausage, available from delicatessens)

12 fresh sage leaves

100 g/4 oz chicken livers, diced

250 ml/8 fl oz dry red wine

about 75 g/3 oz soft white breadcrumbs

For the stuffing, heat the oil in a pan, add the onions, garlic, celery, carrot and thyme and cook gently until softened but not browned. Crumble in the cotechino, add the sage and fry for 10 minutes. Add the chicken livers and cook for 2 minutes. Add the wine and boil until reduced in volume by half. Season with salt and pepper and cool slightly, then stir in enough breadcrumbs to bind. Leave to cool completely.

Stuff the pheasants and wrap each in 2 slices of Parma ham.

Heat half the olive oil in a pan, add the garlic, onion, thyme, chicken livers and chopped porcini and cook until the onion is beginning to soften. Add the mushroom soaking liquid and simmer until it has evaporated.

Heat the remaining olive oil in a roasting tin and brown the birds in it on both sides. Transfer to an oven preheated to its highest setting and roast for 10 minutes. Turn the birds, add the mushroom mixture and the wine and roast for a further 15 minutes.

Remove the birds and keep warm. Set the roasting tin on the hob, stir the juices and whisk in a little butter to enrich them. Serve the birds with the mushroom mixture and juices.

Antony Worrall Thompson Christmas

Roast guinea fowl with thyme, wild mushrooms and garlic bubble and squeak

Guinea fowl is a delicious, tasty, slighty firmer version of chicken. It has a little less fat, so do be careful not to overcook it.

Serves 4

ingredients

2 small fresh thyme sprigs

4 garlic cloves in their skins, lightly crushed

2 guinea fowl

4 tablespoons light olive oil

250 g/9 oz mixed wild mushrooms, such as chanterelles, oysters, shiitake, etc.

salt and freshly ground black pepper

FOR THE BUBBLE AND SQUEAK:

6–8 garlic cloves, unpeeled

2 tablespoons light olive oil

40 g/1½ oz butter

2 tablespoons chopped onion

1 large handful of cooked chopped cabbage

750 g/1 lb 10 oz cooked potatoes

flour for dusting

salt and freshly ground black pepper

FOR THE SAUCE:

100 ml/3½ fl oz Madeira or port

250 ml/8 fl oz brown chicken stock or beef stock

25 g/1 oz cold butter, diced

½ teaspoon fresh thyme leaves (or ¼ teaspoon dried thyme)

½ tablespoon chopped fresh parsley

For the bubble and squeak, place the garlic cloves on a piece of foil and drizzle with 1 tablespoon of the olive oil. Scrunch up the foil into a purse and place in an oven preheated to 180°C/350°F/Gas Mark 4 for 45 minutes. Remove and leave to cool (this can all be done days in advance). Open the foil and carefully squeeze the delicious, mild, creamy garlic from the skins.

Melt two thirds of the butter in a large pan and sauté the onion and cabbage in it for about 3 minutes. Tip it into a large bowl with the garlic. Allow to cool slightly and then add the potatoes. With your hands, mix the ingredients together, crushing the potatoes roughly as you go. Season with salt and pepper. Form the mixture into 4 large balls and dust with flour. Press into neat patties.

Heat the remaining oil and butter in a frying pan and when the butter is foaming add the patties. Cook over a moderate heat for 3–4 minutes on each side. Alternatively, brown them on each side and transfer to a baking sheet. Then they can be reheated when needed.

Place the thyme and garlic inside the guinea fowl. Season inside and out with salt and pepper. Heat 2 tablespoons of the olive oil in a roasting tin in an oven preheated to 200°C/400°F/Gas Mark 6. When it is hot, place the guinea fowl in the tin, on their sides, and roast for 10 minutes. Turn over on to the other side and roast for another 10 minutes. Now turn the guinea fowl breast-side up, turn the oven down to 180°C/350°F/Gas Mark 4 and roast for a further 10 minutes. Remove from the oven and transfer to a warm dish. Cover with foil and leave to rest for 15 minutes.

For the sauce, pour the fat out of the roasting tin, then pour in the Madeira or port and place over a medium heat, stirring and scraping up any juices that may have caramelized on the bottom of the tin. Tip the liquid into a saucepan and add the stock. Boil until reduced by half.

Heat a large frying pan over a high heat and add the remaining olive oil. Fry the mushrooms in it with a little salt for 3–4 minutes, then tip on to a roasting tray and set aside.

With a sharp knife, cut the legs off each bird and place on the roasting tray with the mushrooms. Then carefully cut down each side of the breastbone and remove the breasts. Place on the roasting tray. Save any juices from the birds and add to the sauce.

To serve, warm the mushrooms and guinea fowl in the oven for 3–4 minutes. Bring the sauce to the boil, then whisk in the butter and herbs. Taste for seasoning. (This is a very light sauce. If you prefer a thicker, gravy-style sauce you will need to thicken it.) Reheat the bubble and squeak if necessary. Put the guinea fowl on warmed serving plates and place the mushrooms and bubble and squeak on either side. Pour a little sauce on to each plate.

Tournedos of pork with mashed potato sauce and caramelized apple

Tournedos is a description generally used for beef fillet steak but in this recipe the fillet is created from a leg of pork. The technique breaks down the meat's textures, making it very tender. The pork skin can be cut into thin strips, salted and baked in an oven preheated to 180°C/350°F/Gas Mark 4 for 30 minutes. This will remove all excess fat and leave you with pork crackling. These can be salted and left to cool. A few to eat with the tournedos are lovely.

Serves 8

ingredients

1.5 kg/3½ lb pork from the leg, boned and skin removed (but see above)

10 fresh sage leaves, chopped

225 g/8 oz pig's caul (*crépine*) or 15–18 rashers of smoked streaky bacon (optional)

a knob of butter

salt and freshly ground black pepper

FOR THE MASHED POTATO SAUCE:

600 g/1¼ lb potatoes, preferably Maris Piper or Desiree, peeled and quartered

freshly grated nutmeg

50 g/2 oz butter

150 ml/¼ pint single cream

milk or extra single cream, if needed

Separate the pork into individual muscles by breaking apart the membranes holding them together. Then remove the sinews – or ask your butcher to do it! This will break down the meat even more. It is important that all sinews are totally removed to guarantee the tenderness of the meat. Once all is cleaned, you will have a few meat scraps left over. Mince or process these, making sure you have at least 100 g/4 oz, then season them with salt and pepper and the sage to make a 'farce', or stuffing.

Cut all the remaining meat into strips approximately 10 cm/4 inches long and 1 cm/½ inch wide. Rinse the pig's caul, if using, in cold water to loosen and clean it. If using the bacon rashers simply lay them vertically side by side in a line on a large piece of foil, or use buttered foil on its own. Now lay the strips of pork on the caul, bacon and foil, or foil. Lay them lengthways (in the opposite direction from the bacon) side by side. Spread the 'farce' thinly over the meat and then roll or hand-shape into a cylinder. Wrap tightly in the caul, bacon and foil, or foil, then rewrap in more foil, twisting each end to firm the wrap. Leave to 'set' in the fridge for 1–2 hours.

Cut across the cylinder, still in the foil, into tournedos (fillet steak shapes) 4–5 cm/1½–2 inches thick. This should give you at least 8 portions. If caul or bacon have been used to wrap the meat, remove the outer foil. These portions must now be tied with two pieces of string, to ensure they keep their shape. If only foil has been used, tie string around the outside of it.

For the mashed potato sauce, boil the potatoes in salted water until tender. Drain and replace the lid. Shake the pan vigorously to break up the potatoes. Season with salt,

FOR THE APPLE GRAVY:

300 ml/½ pint apple juice

600 ml/1 pint veal or beef *jus* (or use Crosse & Blackwell's Bonne Cuisine Madeira Wine Gravy, diluted with 450 ml/¾ pint water)

a squeeze of lemon juice (optional)

FOR THE GARNISH:

4 Granny Smith apples, peeled and cored

a knob of butter

a sprinkling of caster sugar

pepper and nutmeg and work in the butter. Warm the cream, then gradually pour into the potato and work until you have a soft dropping and spreading consistency. Check the seasoning and the 'sauce' is ready. If made in advance, you may well find when re-heating it that it has thickened and will need more warm milk or cream to loosen it.

For the apple gravy, boil the apple juice until reduced by two thirds, then add the gravy and reduce to a thick consistency, so it easily coats the back of a spoon. Add a squeeze of lemon juice, if you like, to sharpen the flavour.

For the garnish, cut through the middle of each apple and trim off the ends, to give slices 1–2 cm/½–¾ inch thick.

Season the pork tournedos and sauté in the butter until nicely browned on all sides. Cook in an oven preheated to 200°C/400°F/Gas Mark 6 for 12–15 minutes to finish cooking. This will leave the pork still moist in the centre. Leave to rest for 5–6 minutes. Meanwhile, fry the apple slices in butter for 5–6 minutes, until golden and tender. Then sit them on a baking tray, wider-side up, and sprinkle with caster sugar. Caramelize under a hot grill.

To serve, remove the string and any foil from the pork. Spoon some warm mashed potato sauce on the top half of each plate. Place the apples towards the front with the pork tournedos sitting at the side. Add some crackling if you've made this. Trickle on the apple gravy and serve.

Timpano di lasagne al duca d'este

Timpano of lasagne with fillets of sole and shrimps

In Italy a fish pasta dish is traditional on Christmas Eve.

Serves 6–8

ingredients

500 g/1 lb 2 oz raw shrimps or prawns, peeled and shells reserved

500 ml/17 fl oz water

250 ml/8 fl oz dry white wine

1 small onion, roughly chopped

2 bay leaves

5 black peppercorns

250 g/9 oz butter, plus extra for finishing

500 g/1 lb 2 oz Dover sole, filleted

1 measure of brandy

50 g/2 oz plain flour

100 g/4 oz Parmesan cheese, freshly grated

salt and freshly ground black pepper

FOR THE PASTA:

350 g/12 oz type '0' flour or strong white flour (or '00' flour if using an electric pasta machine)

3 eggs

First make the pasta: put the flour in a mound and make a hollow in the centre. Add a little salt to the eggs, beat lightly and pour into the hollow. Draw the flour into the eggs until well amalgamated. If the mixture is too moist, add a little more flour. Knead the dough with the heel of the palm of your hand, keeping your fingers bent, folding the pasta in half and giving it a half turn. Do this for 10 minutes. Cut the pasta into 12.5 cm/5 inch squares, and lay them on tea towels to dry for an hour before boiling.

Put the pasta in a large pan of boiling salted water and when it rises to the top, drain and dip straight away into a bowl of cold water. Drain again and lay out on tea towels.

Put the prawn or shrimp shells in a pan with the water, half the wine, the onion, bay leaves and peppercorns and bring to a gentle boil. Reduce the heat and simmer for 10 minutes, crushing the shells occasionally. Strain the stock, pressing the shells down well to extract as much flavour as possible.

Heat 100 g/4 oz of the butter in a pan, then gently fry the sole fillets in it. Season and add the remaining wine. Cook for a few minutes until the sauce has thickened, then set aside. Sauté the shrimps or prawns in 75 g/3 oz of the butter, pour over the brandy and ignite. Set aside.

Melt the remaining butter over a low heat. Add the flour and mix in thoroughly, then gradually add the reserved shrimp/prawn stock. Bring the sauce gently to the boil, stirring with a balloon whisk, and cook for about 10 minutes, always stirring, until the sauce looks silky. Remove from the heat and stir in the Parmesan.

Butter a gratin dish. Add a layer of pasta, sprinkle on some shrimps or prawns with some of the cooking juices, then a little fish stock béchamel. Follow with a layer of pasta and press down, then scatter the sole fillets with some of their cooking juices and more béchamel. Continue layering, finishing with a layer of pasta topped with the remaining béchamel. Dot with flecks of butter and bake in an oven preheated to 180°C/350°F/Gas Mark 4 for 30 minutes or until the top has a beautiful golden crust.

Shorvedar khumbi

Mushroom curry

I have used ordinary white mushrooms here but you may make this with almost any seasonal mushrooms. Whichever kind you get, cut them into large, chunky pieces so they do not get lost in the sauce.

Serves 4

ingredients

4 cm/1½ inch piece fresh ginger, peeled and chopped

115 g/4 oz onions, peeled and chopped

3 cloves garlic, peeled and chopped

450 g/1 lb large mushrooms

6 tablespoons vegetable oil

3 tablespoon natural yoghurt

1 teaspoon tomato purée

2 teaspoons ground coriander

½ teaspoon salt

⅛–¼ teaspoon chilli powder

2 tablespoons chopped green coriander

Put the ginger, onion and garlic into the container of an electric blender along with 3 tablespoons water and blend until smooth.

Wipe the mushrooms with a damp cloth and cut them into halves or quarters, depending upon size. Put 3 tablespoons of the oil in a non-stick frying pan and set over high heat. When hot, put in the mushrooms. Stir and fry for 2–3 minutes or until the mushrooms have lost their raw look. Empty the contents of the pan into a bowl. Wipe the pan.

Put the remaining 3 tablespoons oil into the pan and set over high heat. When hot, put in the paste from the blender. Stir and fry for 3–4 minutes, until it starts turning brown. Add 1 tablespoon of the yoghurt and fry for 30 seconds. Add another tablespoon of the yoghurt and fry for 30 seconds. Do this a third time. Now put in the tomato purée and fry for 30 seconds. Put in the ground coriander and stir once or twice. Now put in 300 ml/10 fl oz water, the mushrooms and their juices, salt and chilli powder. Stir and bring to a simmer. Turn the heat to low and simmer for 5 minutes. Sprinkle the green coriander over the top before serving.

Madhur Jaffrey Christmas

Cranberry and baked pear pancakes with Calvados cream

Serves 4

ingredients

65 g/2½ oz plain flour

150 ml/¼ pint milk

1 egg, lightly beaten

½ teaspoon oil

a little melted butter to grease the pan

icing sugar for dusting

berries and mint or holly leaves, to decorate

FOR THE CALVADOS CREAM:

250 ml/8 fl oz milk

½ vanilla pod, split in half lengthways

2 large egg yolks

50 g/2 oz caster sugar

75 ml/2½ fl oz double cream

2 tablespoons Calvados

FOR THE FILLING:

75 g/3 oz fresh cranberries

25 g/1 oz butter

4 William pears, peeled, cored and cut into 5 mm/¼ inch pieces

100 ml/3½ fl oz white wine

juice of 1 orange

¼ cinnamon stick

1 tablespoon caster sugar

1 tablespoon apricot jam

First make the Calvados cream: put the milk in a heavy-based saucepan, add the vanilla pod and bring to the boil. Beat the egg yolks with the sugar until slightly foamy, then gradually add the hot milk, whisking constantly. Pour back into the pan and heat slowly, stirring with a wooden spoon. Do not let it boil or the mixture will separate. Continue to heat slowly, stirring, until the sauce thickens enough to coat the back of the spoon. Immediately remove from the heat and strain through a fine sieve. Stir the cream into the mixture, followed by the Calvados.

To make the pancakes, sift the flour into a bowl and whisk in the milk, egg and oil. Cover and leave to rest for 10 minutes.

Brush a non-stick frying pan with melted butter. Add a quarter of the pancake batter (about 4 tablespoons) and swirl the pan round so that it coats it evenly. Cook until the underside is golden, then turn and cook the other side. Remove from the pan and set aside. Repeat with the remaining batter to make 4 pancakes altogether. Do not lay them on top of each other or they will stick.

To make the filling, cook the cranberries in boiling water for 2 minutes, then drain and set aside. Heat the butter in a pan, add the pears and cranberries and sweat for about 1 minute. Add the white wine, orange juice, cinnamon stick and sugar. Bring to the boil and simmer until the pear is tender. Strain the liquid through a sieve into a pan. Set aside the pear and cranberry mixture and remove the cinnamon stick. Bring the liquid to the boil, add the apricot jam and boil until reduced by half, then stir into the pear and cranberry mixture.

Gently reheat the Calvados cream if necessary. Place the filling in the centre of each pancake. Fold in about 2.5 cm/1 inch at each end, then roll each into a cigar shape. Place in a heatproof dish and sprinkle with the icing sugar. Place under a preheated grill to brown. Decorate the pancakes with fresh berries and mint or holly leaves. Serve with the Calvados cream.

Torta di cioccolata

Chocolate torte

Serves 8

ingredients

150 g/5 oz whole blanched almonds

1 × 2 cm/¾ inch slice of panettone

165 g/5½ oz unsalted butter

300 g/10½ oz good-quality plain chocolate

150 g/5 oz caster sugar

4 eggs

½ vanilla pod

150 g/5 oz mascarpone cheese

Combine the almonds and panettone in a food processor and whizz until they form a fine meal. Rub an 18 cm/ 7 inch round springform cake tin generously with 15 g/ ½ oz of the butter and sprinkle with some of the almond mixture. Roll the mixture around to form an even coating, then invert the tin to shake out excess nuts and panettone crumbs.

Melt the chocolate with 2 tablespoons of water in a double boiler or a microwave. While it is melting, cream the remaining butter and the sugar in a food processor. Add the eggs, the scraped-out vanilla seeds, melted chocolate, remaining nut and panettone mixture and the mascarpone. Whizz until just incorporated, no more. Pour and scrape into the prepared cake tin and bake in an oven preheated to 180°C/350°F/Gas Mark 4 for about 40 minutes. The cake should be just about set: cracks will appear about 2 cm/¾ inch from the rim and when they have spread all around the cake in a circle this is a pretty certain indication that it is done. Remove from the oven and leave for 20 minutes before unmoulding. The cake is best served warm, when it may be a little runny in the middle.

Baked Christmas Alaska

Serves 6

ingredients

300 g/10½ oz caster sugar

4 tablespoons brandy

1 × 20 cm/8 inch Victoria sponge cake, sliced horizontally in 3

450 ml/¾ pint vanilla ice cream, slightly softened

200 g/7 oz Christmas pudding

4 egg whites

Put 50 g/2 oz of the sugar in a small pan with 200 ml/ 7 fl oz water and heat gently to dissolve the sugar. Bring to the boil, simmer for a few minutes to make a syrup, then leave to cool. Stir in 3 tablespoons of the brandy.

Place one of the sponge layers on a baking tray and brush with some of the syrup. Mix the ice cream and Christmas pudding together and place in the centre of the sponge, heaping it up in a mound and leaving a 1 cm/½ inch border all round. Cut the remaining sponge layers into triangles and use to cover the entire Christmas pudding ice cream. Brush with the remaining syrup and place in the freezer until very firm.

Put the remaining caster sugar in a pan with 4 tablespoons of water and heat gently until dissolved, then boil rapidly for 1 minute. In an electric mixer, whisk the egg whites until stiff, then slowly pour in the dissolved sugar, whisking constantly. Continue to whisk until the meringue is completely cool and very stiff.

Place the meringue in a piping bag and pipe it all over the Christmas Alaska as quickly as possible, making a little hollow at the top. Bake in an oven preheated to 220°C/425°F/Gas Mark 7 for 5 minutes, until brown. Warm the remaining brandy. Pour it into the hollow at the top of the baked Alaska and ignite carefully with a match. Serve immediately.

Sicilian cassata

Serves 6

ingredients

500 g/1 lb 2 oz very fresh ricotta cheese

300 g/10½ oz icing sugar, sifted

1 teaspoon vanilla extract

3 tablespoons rum or liqueur

3 tablespoons good-quality plain chocolate, cut into splinters

3 tablespoons chopped mixed candied peel

600 g/1½ lb plain sponge cake, thinly sliced

6 tablespoons custard (from a carton is fine)

3 tablespoons apricot jam

pale green ready-to-roll icing

TO DECORATE (SELECT FROM THE FOLLOWING:

flakes of chocolate, candied fruit, glacé fruit, silver balls, sugared almonds, rice paper flowers, coloured dragees

Push the ricotta through a sieve, then blend it with the icing sugar until it is the consistency of lightly whipped cream. Flavour it with the vanilla extract and rum or liqueur. Mix in the chocolate splinters and candied peel.

Line a 1.75 litre/3 pint bowl or pudding basin with aluminium foil or clingfilm, then line it with slices of sponge cake, using a little of the custard to cement them together securely. Place a layer of sponge in the bottom of the bowl, cover with some custard and then some of the ricotta mixture. Repeat these layers, ending with sponge. Put a plate on top and weight it down, then chill for about 2–3 hours.

Turn the cassata out on to a plate. Warm the apricot jam until it is runny and then brush it over the sponge. Cover with the icing. Decorate it as much as possible to make it look like the wonderfully baroque Sicilian dessert that is famous all over the world. Chill until required.

Index

Index